"Authority over The Nations" GOD and Politics

God bless you Aileen & Lewis.

[signature]

13. 7. 19.

"Authority over The Nations" GOD and Politics

By Sidney Cordle MBE

Includes the Christian Peoples Alliance Manifesto

Published by
SERVANT BOOKS
Godsoyster@aol.com

DEDICATION

This book is dedicated to the 30 candidates who stood with me in the 2017 General Election for the CPA

Stephen Todd
Robin Rennie
Venetia Sams
Morenike Mafoh
Angel Watt
Helen Spiby-Vann
Kayode Shedowo
Malcolm Martin
Maureen Martin
Ray Towey
Katherine Hortense
John Boadu
David Omamogho
Des Coke
Ashley Dickinson

Steve Benson
Faith Fisher
Iris White
Temitope Olodo
Chine Nwabikedu
Kemi Abidogun
Rose Domain
Abiola Ajoku
Roger Peacock
John Wesley Gibson
Edmonds Victor
Lorna Corke
John Allman
Tim Mutamiri
Alex Coetzee

Contents

ACKNOWLEDGEMENTS

I owe a debt of gratitude to so many. First of all, to my wonderful wife Bukky. Before we got married ministry together was powerful. Since then we have taken each other to new levels ministering together in different places and honouring each other's calling. What is most pleasant is there is no sense of competition! We just honour what God does through the other and each is happy to sit back and listen or go to the front and minister as the need demands and above all pray for each other at all times. Bukky's support for my political calling is total and that means far more than she knows. I also honour all my children and grandchildren God has given. As I often say, when you set out in life you never know what is going to be your lot. I certainly didn't set out intending to get divorced. However, it led me over time to appreciate my three children Alexandra, Emily and Jo more than ever and I am becoming also very fond of my grandchildren Ella, Bethann and Susanna. I love being with each one of you. Re-marrying has also made me step dad to four more children one of whom Ruben I have had the honour of living with and caring for with Bukky. Ruben you are a great joy! Finally, there is Zahra our adopted daughter who we met through ministry. She has been a tremendous support and encouragement and it is a pleasure to walk with her.

Acknowledgements

To Dr Chris Atkins I would like to say thank you for standing with me in the dark times. Those hikes on the moors when we could just talk mean more than you know. To John O'Brien, your total dedication to revival and deep commitment to prayer and listening to worship music and love for children has been a tremendous inspiration. To Flora Amar, your dedication to listening to God and belief that God's anointing is over the CPA and God will raise up this party and willingness to communicate that vision has sustained me powerfully. To Robin Jegede-Brimson, it's been an honour to be connected and to see your total commitment to obey whatever God says no matter what it costs and to walk in the prophetic with you. Thank you for honouring me. To Prophet Johnson Akinfenwa, thank you for speaking at the CPA Assembly 2018 and sharing the Satanic Agenda and thank you for being willing to listen to God and speak out His word with boldness and lead so many people in praying for the nation. Your work must be rewarded! To Jay Smith, thank you for teaching me so much about Islam. It was a pleasure working with you and thank you for devoting your life to undermining the historical basis of the Islamic religion academically and publicly, fearlessly, confronting Islam with your research. To all the thirty-one candidates who stood in 2017 for the CPA, thank you for your dedication to stand for God. Of special note is Malcolm Martin who as my deputy eased the burden tremendously, Roger Peacock who did likewise and showed tremendous generosity and Lorna Corke who as President has prayed with me regularly and shown a depth in her relationship with God the whole world needs. To Richard and Liz Mitchell, thank you for standing so boldly and strongly for the Lord no matter what obstacles you face. You shall both yet live for many years to see fulfilled the vision God has prepared. To Jonathan and Abbih Oloyede, thank you for listening to God and giving us opportunities to lead and minister. To all the precious people at City Chapel Beckton and especially Sam Bankole, God gave us something very special that will be never be lost and you were part of it. To Denis Greenidge, it's an honour to be connected and thank you for your passion to follow God no matter where it leads. To all my friends in IPAA I love being with you and ministering together; God has given us something very precious and special which will bear fruit for eternity. There are many more I could mention so finally to all my other friends and family not mentioned here, thank you. God hasn't yet begun to pour out the fullness. So far we have only gone ankle deep. More is coming!

Acknowledgements

INTRODUCTION

Sid Cordle was born into a family where his father's cousin was a member of Parliament, John Cordle, MP for Bournemouth. Among the MP's children Anthony Cordle who Sid met in 1979 was used by God to set up the Parliamentary Prayer Breakfast with others. People still ask Sid "are you related to Anthony Cordle?" His Grandfather on his mother's side was a Councillor and his mother declared that the only reason he wasn't an MP was he wasn't rich enough. All this political interest seemed to come together in Sid. He remembers when he was seven his grandfather was standing in a Council election. He wanted to go out and put some leaflets through doors for him and go and talk to people about voting for him. Sid stood for his school Council aged fifteen and won. As soon as he got to University, he stood for the Union Council and won a seat. In his final year he stood for Union President, coming second out of four candidates, all this time standing just as a Christian in politics. He went to NUS Conferences and found every shade of left-wing opinion under the sun expressed but no Christian stall at all. With the help of UCCF he put that right. He became the national co-ordinator of Christians in Student Politics and ran bookstalls at all NUS Conferences and also fringe meetings for Christians and separate Conferences. For a long time, he felt that period was the most productive of his life. When he left

University however, he felt he couldn't be effective as a lone Christian voice in the big wide world of politics, so he needed to join a mainstream party. His politics was very influenced by the persecution of Christians behind the iron curtain under Communism. His young heart hated the fact his brothers and sisters had Bibles taken from them and if they held any sort of meeting were beaten up or imprisoned for it. What sort of people were these Communists? He found them at University and boldly challenged them at every opportunity. The Labour Party was never going to be a party for him. Then a friend of his scoffed at the Liberals and advised him the only party he could join was the Conservatives. Thus, one day in December 1977 he turned up at the Conservative Office in Sheffield and said he wanted to join. He was allocated to a branch and immediately went out knocking on doors.

His degree was Biblical Studies. At this time, he wanted to go into the church but didn't know how it would fit in with his political interest. He needed to work first somewhere and see what God was calling him to do. Because he had been campaigning for Union President in his final year, he hadn't had time to look for a career, so he finished University without a job. He was desperate to work and eventually took his first job as an insurance agent with the Prudential in January 1978. He had always been good with figures. He found he had a job where he could earn a decent living working 25 to 30 hours a week. This left time for him to campaign which he duly did.

His enthusiasm for politics was such that a Conservative Ward in the East of the city heard about him and asked him to be their candidate in the May 1978 local elections. Armed with leaflets he went out putting them through doors and knocking on doors. It was a time when the Conservative Party was at its height with a very unpopular Labour Government that had just gone on its knees to the IMF to bail out the country. He won support never dreamed of before in that area but not enough to get elected. It was a solid Labour area.

He was duly invited to campaign in an area closer to where he lived. The political tide started to turn but his hard work got noticed. A Conservative Councillor died in 1982 and he was asked to be the candidate for the ward. He was subsequently elected in July 1982 in a by election to Sheffield City Council. He was part of a group of eighteen Conservative Councillors out of seventy in a Labour dominated city. Prior to his first Council meeting a taxi arrived with all the papers. He read them assiduously. What particularly caught his eye were two notices of motion. One was in support of a steel strike, the other in support of a strike at a firm called Electronic Data Processing. It so happened that among his Prudential clients was a shop steward in the steel works so Sid quizzed him as to what was going on and found out all he needed to know. For the EDP dispute Sid had to ring the firm and get information that way.

He arrived at his first Conservative Group meeting, two days before the Council meeting, armed with all this information. These items were listed to be discussed at the end of the agenda, but they were put there by the Labour Party who had a clear majority on the Council. Unknown to Sid it was normal practice for them to move to have their motions debated at the start of the meeting, so they would get more press attention. This gave the motions much greater importance. His knowledge was such that the group asked him to second an amendment proposed by the Conservative Group leader on the steel strike and to propose an amendment on the EDP dispute as no-one else at the meeting knew anything about it at all. Sid therefore arrived at his first meeting, was introduced as a new Councillor and shook hands with the Lord Mayor. The first item was the steel strike. David Blunkett then leader of the Council, later Home Secretary, moved the motion. The Conservative leader, David Heslop, moved the amendment. Sid was then invited to second the amendment, the third speaker of the meeting. By this time, he was also on the executive of the National Union of Insurance Workers. The Labour Party had never before had a trade unionist on the

Conservative side who knew so much about an industrial dispute! Half an hour later came the EDP resolution. He was the second speaker; "this Council has a legal responsibility to run schools in this city, to provide Council Housing, to clear refuse and sweep the streets, to provide Libraries and Parks. We are raising the rates by enormous amounts. If instead of focusing on the provision of services this Council instead spends its money on supporting strikes it has no responsibility for whatsoever but which are in fact destroying good businesses, the time will come when the people of this city will start refusing to pay their rates (now Council tax) and I will be at the forefront of organising it." David Blunkett rose to his feet. "Who is this new Councillor? Is this new Councillor telling people to break the law? I think we should call this Councillor Sid Vicious". Next day the headline of the local paper was "Sid is so Vicious". But he made enemies that day on his own side. One in particular was jealous that he had taken the limelight as he did at his first meeting.

It took a while before he was accepted and given responsibility. Still by the time he left, after six years, he had led a successful campaign to save sixth forms in the Conservative part of the city, the Council wanted to close, and as shadow chairman of planning had helped get planning permission for Meadowhall, a massive new out of town shopping area, the developer having taken advice from Sid before he spoke to anyone from the Council. In the midst of this activity he stood for Parliament in 1983 in Sheffield Heeley. Had they not changed the boundaries he would have won the seat and been one of the youngest MPs in Parliament. As it was it was just beyond him, but he campaigned very hard. He left the Council in 1988 now with 2 young children and a third soon to come. He was duly rewarded with an MBE in the New Year's Honours List 1989 for all his hard work. It is very unusual for a thirty-two-year-old to be given such an honour for public and political service. He went for a safe Conservative seat in 1987 but didn't get selected. He campaigned in 1992 in Sheffield Hillsborough having gone all over the country trying to get a good seat but failing. The constituency chairman reported Sid was "by far the best candidate we've ever had". His business life hit turmoil in 1996 that led him to leave the Prudential and set up as an Independent Financial Adviser. He worked with a colleague for a year and then set up his own business in 1997. All this didn't allow him to stand in the 1997 election.

His home life then fell apart from late 1998 throughout 1999 culminating in a very nasty divorce in 2000 and court cases in 2001 to sort out the finances. All this prevented him from standing in 2001. At this time, he couldn't see his children (March 2000 to August 2003) and he felt as though he were going through a dark tunnel. In it he met God powerfully.

He saw videos of the revival going on in Toronto, so he said "I need God. I'm going there." In June 2002 he duly got on a Canada Airways flight and flew to Toronto. He stayed with a family from the church who were lovely and went to the Toronto Airport Christian Fellowship. His first meeting was a Tuesday night, his last Sunday morning. In between were three meetings a day, a total of fourteen meetings altogether and Sid didn't miss even part of one. He met two wonderful Americans there who kept praying for him, Jim and Karen West. In their words, "when we first met Sid, he seemed so sad, but his face just lit up more and more as the week went on." Standing in Toronto he felt as though God was standing next to him and he felt totally forgiven for all he'd ever done. Before Sid had his security in being a husband, having three lovely children, living in a nice house, being a pastoral leader in the church, chairman of the residents' association. He had all that taken away from him, but he found his security again in just being a child of God and knowing his Heavenly Father loved him. That is something no-one can ever take away, ever. The final Sunday he was given a prophetic word: "You are precious to me, I love you my child. I will prosper you abundantly. Stay in me, do not despair. I will make my way clear to you." As he heard it given to him he broke down in tears and received it all. He came away vowing "I will do anything you want God. I don't care what it is so long as I know it's your will. You have to be clear. I don't want to make mistakes."

Introduction

Not long after this he went to a candidate selection panel to be a Conservative Candidate in the 2005 General Election. By now Ian Duncan Smith had been ousted and Michael Howard had taken over as leader of the Conservative Party. Ian Duncan Smith had a 3-line whip against homosexual couples being allowed to adopt children. Theresa May as his party chairman gave a speech about it at the Conference Sid was at, saying "we are being perceived as the nasty party". Rebellion was in the air. Michael Howard came in saying "people choose to live their lives differently these days and we have to adapt our policies accordingly." Sid knew what that meant. Out with Christian family values and in with liberal social values. Before the selection meeting he prayed with his second cousin Anthony. He then stood outside the hotel and declared "God I am not going into this place to compromise to get accepted. If your presence will not go with me I will not go up from here." It is an exhaustive process but by this time he was very experienced. Everything went fine until it came to the individual interview. Then the MP asked him "What change would you most like to see in the country?" Without hesitating he replied "revival". "What's that?" he asked. Sid told him it's where large numbers of people become Christians and incredible miracles take place. Silence. He knew instantly that he had failed the selection and that was how it turned out. He passed every part except the individual interview. It also turned out that where before the Conservative Party allowed local candidates Michael Howard was now determined not to allow anyone to stand for the party not approved by the central board. He was stuck.

Shortly after this Sid was at a Conference where he met Jill McLaughlin who had been part of a prayer group for the nation, he was involved in. He told her his story. "Why don't you stand for the Christian Peoples Alliance?" she said. He replied, "I've never heard of that Party, but I will pray and see what God says". Before Sid now was the dream of his youth, just standing for God in politics. He had been quite happy in the Conservative Party but now the Party had changed course. One door was closed but suddenly another was open. Is this your will God? "Yes". "God says Yes", "Jill, God says yes, I am to join the CPA". He joined early 2004 and immediately helped Ram Gidoomal campaigning for London mayor. He also got elected to the Executive of the CPA and was CPA candidate for Sheffield Hallam in 2005 where he had been a Councillor. He worked phenomenally hard and spent an enormous amount of money on the campaign but got no-where. This was very different from campaigning for the Conservative Party. Seeing how hard he had worked Alan Craig, then a Councillor for the CPA in Canning Town, invited him to come and work with him in London. Sid realised that he was detached from the main party and couldn't make progress staying in Sheffield. He duly started campaigning in London with his usual gusto. First, he gave up 2 weeks in August 2005 to knock on doors full time, then he started coming down weekends. For a while he was in Sheffield doing his financial advice Monday to Friday then Friday, he would get a train lunchtime to London where he would knock on doors all day Saturday, go to a church Sunday and a meeting Monday morning then back to Sheffield. By 4pm he would be back at his desk in Sheffield and seeing clients in the evening. By Tuesday he was exhausted, but he adapted to it. In 2008 he bought a house in London to make the process easier and another in 2011. Alan Craig stood down as CPA leader in October 2012 and Sid was elected leader by postal ballot in December 2012. He remembers coming away from the office where the votes had been counted exhilarated "I am leader of the CPA." The party had never had a leader with such political experience. Where could we go now? Since then progress has been slower than he hoped but his initial aim of moving the party from decline to growth has certainly happened. Everything is now growing; finance, enthusiasm, candidates, membership. We are building towards Government. We are joining with the Christian Party to have one united Christian voice in the nation and we are seeking to work with the DUP. We pray for an hour before every meeting and we spend 30 mins. on the phone praying every week. God is directing us, and God is in charge.

Surely a party 100% devoted to God has to be blessed doesn't it?

Introduction

CHAPTER 1
The Call to Engage

"If you set out to be liked, you would be prepared to compromise on anything at any time, and you would achieve nothing."

Margaret Thatcher

The Call to Engage

We are told that the Father judges no-one but has given all judgement to the Son. We are told the Son will judge nations. "When the Son of Man comes in His glory, and all the angels with Him, He will sit on His glorious throne. All the nations will be gathered before Him, and He will separate the people one from another as a shepherd separates the sheep from the goats. He will put the sheep on his right and the goats on his left. Then the King will say to those on his right, 'Come, you who are blessed by my Father; take your inheritance, the kingdom prepared for you since the creation of the world...'" (Mt 25:31f.)

So, there are sheep nations and goat nations. But what has this got to do with us? Many Christians feel we should focus on sharing the gospel to non-believers and not worry about politics. But if we do that we are missing out. First Psalm 2 tells us that there are nations conspiring against God and he laughs at them. God then says, "Ask me, and I will make the nations your inheritance, the ends of the earth your possession. You will break them with a rod of iron; you will dash them to pieces like pottery."

So, we can ask and thereby take charge of nations. Jesus however takes this one step further. He quotes this Psalm when he is speaking to the church in Thyatira and the message is just amazing. It starts with a warning, "I have this against you: You tolerate that woman Jezebel, (Note it says "tolerate" in the church not "engage with") who calls herself a prophet. By her teaching she misleads my servants into sexual immorality and the eating of food sacrificed to idols. I have given her time to repent of her immorality, but she is unwilling." Jesus then continues, "Now I say to the rest of you in Thyatira, to you who do not hold to her teaching and have not learned Satan's so-called deep secrets, (so those who do not tolerate sexual immorality.) 'I will not impose any other burden on you, except to hold on to what you have until I come.' To the one who is victorious and does my will to the end, I will give authority over the nations— that one 'will rule them with an iron sceptre and will dash them to pieces like pottery'—just as I have received authority from my Father. I will also give that one the morning star."

So, Jesus is saying that in the same way as He has authority from the Father to judge nations, so He gives us authority over nations provided we are pure and holy and don't tolerate sexual immorality. But this is not for individuals. This is for the church of God, Christians standing together in unity. He also says I will "give that one the morning star". Is 14:12 says, "How you have fallen from heaven, morning star, son of the dawn! You have been cast down to the earth, you who once laid low the nations!" This is Satan, referred to as the morning star. Jesus is referred to as the bright morning star in Revelation 22:16 but only Satan as the morning star. So, Jesus is saying you can have authority over the nations in the same way as I have authority and you can control Satan. Now who wouldn't want that?

It's time to start seeing how we can put this into practice. This book will examine what it will look like when Christians start to walk in this authority.

The book is unashamedly about politics but it's not about how Christians can perhaps have some influence in a secular party. This isn't about Conservative Christians or Christians on the left although we look at those options in chapter 5. This is about placing God first in the political realm far above every other doctrine or philosophy. It's about seeking His heart and His will without reservation.

Before we go further though we need to face some obstacles head on.

For a long time, Christian thinking on politics has been dominated by the discourse in Mt 22.17-22. The Pharisees asked Jesus "what is your opinion? Is it right to pay the imperial tax to Caesar or not?" But Jesus, knowing their evil intent, said, "You hypocrites, why are you trying to trap me? Show me the coin used for paying the tax." They brought him a denarius, and he asked them, "Whose image is this? And whose inscription?" "Caesar's," they replied. Then he said to them, "So give back to Caesar what is Caesar's, and to God what is God's." When they heard this, they were amazed. So, they left him and went away." So, what was Jesus saying?

The traditional interpretation is that there is a realm which is Caesar's which is politics and the State and there is a realm which is God's which is church and personal faith and the two are separate and should not mix. Some say, "Here is the separation of church and State taught by Jesus." However, there is a problem with this interpretation.

First it is hard to define what this realm is that God isn't interested in. Is it just anything to do with tax? Or is it any laws passed by Parliament? But what about when Parliament passes laws to kill babies in their mother's womb? What about when Parliament passes laws to re-define marriage and says a man and a man can marry? Are these things God isn't interested in? Certainly not. And no Christian can sit easily with the idea God isn't interested in money.

Second it contradicts the Old Testament which His hearers would have been very familiar with. Psalm 24:1 says "The earth is the Lord's, and everything in it, the world, and all who live in it."

Psalm 103:19 says "The Lord has established his throne in heaven, and His kingdom rules over all." Psalm 46:8-10, "Come and see what the Lord has done, the desolations He has brought on the earth. He makes wars cease to the ends of the earth. He breaks the bow and shatters the spear; He burns the shields with fire. He says, "Be still, and know that I am God; I will be exalted among the nations, I will be exalted in the earth." None of these verses allow for a realm that God is not interested in called the State.

Then third it contradicts other, things Jesus Himself said. Jesus said "No one can serve two masters. Either you will hate the one and love the other, or you will be devoted to the one and despise the other. You cannot serve both God and money." If you can't serve 2 masters how can you serve God and the State which are two separate powers and therefore 2 masters and how can God not be interested in tax? Then Jesus tells us to pray "your kingdom come, your will be done, on earth as it is in heaven." That is totally all encompassing. There is no realm in heaven that God is not in charge of and Jesus says we should pray for the same realm to operate on the earth.

It's easier therefore to believe that Jesus wasn't talking about a separate realm He is not interested in. But if this is right then suddenly Christians can get their hands dirty and be involved in politics again, not as seeking to influence some dirty world but as seeking to see God's kingdom rule in every sphere of life.

That does just leave the question what did Jesus mean then? It is believed Jesus was saying "Let Caesar have his money. God will take care of you." This fits with Jesus overall message of holiness and purity which is a theme which flows through this book. Anything not of God has to be removed. The Greek word Jesus uses, _απόδοτε_ (apodote) means to yield, let go of. He was telling the Jews to get rid of things that are not sanctified by God and do not emanate from Him and that includes Caesar's coins. We could also reflect on what Jesus meant when he said "O Jerusalem, Jerusalem, the one who kills the prophets and stones those who are sent to her! How often I wanted to gather your children together, as a hen gathers her chicks under her wings, but you were not willing." (Mt.23:37) Jesus wanted to guard and protect Jerusalem from all the hostile external forces. No doubt that included the Romans. Because they did not receive Jesus's protection Jerusalem was made desolate by the Romans in 70AD as Jesus prophesied. Now a statement that they could stop using Caesar's money and then he no longer has power over them would lead his hearers to be amazed and also on another occasion cause the people to try and grab Jesus and make him their king. There is no reason to be amazed about a statement, "God isn't interested in Caesar. Let him do what he wants."

Someone might then turn me to Romans 13, so we will also address that. It says, "Let everyone be subject to the governing authorities, for there is no authority except that which God has established. The authorities that exist have been established by God. Consequently, whoever rebels against the authority is rebelling against what God has instituted, and those who do so will bring judgment on themselves. For rulers hold no terror for those who do right, but for those who do wrong. Do you want to be free from fear of the one in authority? Then do what is right and you will be commended. For the one in authority is God's servant for your good. But if you do wrong, be afraid, for rulers do not bear the sword for no reason. They are God's servants, agents of wrath to bring punishment on the wrongdoer. Therefore, it is necessary to submit to the authorities." This passage would appear to be directly contrary to the separation of church and State philosophy but has its own challenges.

Jesus also says something similar to Pilate. Pilate says, "Do you refuse to speak to me? Don't you realize I have power either to free you or to crucify you?" Jesus answered, "You would have no power over me if it were not given to you from above." So, Jesus is saying the political authority that Pilate has is given from above and Paul says that rulers have authority from God. You might well ask, "But what if my ruler is Stalin who is telling me not to pray or go to church at the penalty of death?" The command to "do what is right" is never ever surpassed. If rulers are telling you to worship false gods as indeed Shadrach, Meshach, and Abednego were told to, then God will meet you at your place of defying that instruction. It is the instruction that must be changed. However, you are never to engage in revolt or rebellion. We are always called to seek peaceful change so far as is possible and, in a democracy, peaceful change is easy. In fact, to a certain degree this is encouraging Christians to be involved in politics because it says God is choosing rulers and surely, He wants His people to be available to choose from. God cannot choose people completely ill equipped to lead the nation.

So, from this point on we work in the belief that God's will does indeed encompass every aspect of life including the political sphere and we will begin to study what it's like for God to have authority over our nation as well as other nations of the earth. Now we are not asking for individual Christians to stand alone in the political sphere. It is sometimes suggested that Christians should stand as independents. No sorry, that is not Godly. We are calling for God's people to move in and take over this realm as a mighty army with God totally at the head of everything we say and do. What will this look like?

The Call to Engage

CHAPTER 2

The Context and The foundation

"I build on Christ, the rock of ages; on his sure mercies described in his word, and on his promises, all which I know are yea and amen."

John Wesley

The Context

The first thing we need to grasp is a little bit of what it means when Paul talks about "the mystery that has been kept hidden for ages and generations but is now disclosed to the Lord's people. To them God has chosen to make known among the Gentiles the glorious riches of this mystery." What is this mystery? "Christ in you, the hope of glory." (Colossians 1:26,27).

This mystery of Christ in you is often interpreted as applying to individual Christians but that is not what Paul is talking about here. The context is verse 24, "Now I rejoice in what I am suffering for you, and I fill up in my flesh what is still lacking in regard to Christ's afflictions, for the sake of his body, which is the church." He is talking about the church. The mystery disclosed to the Lord's people is of Christ dwelling in His church.

Likewise, Paul says in Ephesians 2 "You are...fellow citizens with God's people and also members of his household, built on the foundation of the apostles and prophets, with Christ Jesus himself as the chief cornerstone. In him the whole building is joined together and rises to become a holy temple in the Lord. And in him you too are being built together to become a dwelling in which God lives by his

Spirit." So, the dwelling place has a shape and a structure. The foundation is apostles and prophets, those called by God to lead and to listen to His voice. Jesus Christ himself is the cement and the mainstay of the building. Every church member is meant to be cemented into the structure. It then becomes a holy temple where the Spirit of God lives.

So, God's plan is that He dwells with His people who are in unity and His temple is in His church.

Now please don't misunderstand this. Paul says, "do you not know that your body is the temple of the Holy Spirit, which is in you, whom you have received from God." (1 Corinthians .6:19). On the day of Pentecost, they were all filled with the Holy Spirit. The Holy Spirit does indeed dwell in each of us individually. But there is something about the manifestation of the glory of God which seems to be reserved for the church dwelling in prayer and purity and unity worshipping God.

God calls us always to press in to know more of Him and receive more of Him. I think that is why often we don't get quick answers to our prayers. He wants us to be in that place where we are desperate for more.

But the prize is just awesome. Solomon experienced it when he finished building the temple and worshipped there. "Fire came down from heaven and consumed the burnt offering and the sacrifices; and the glory of the LORD filled the temple. And the priests could not enter the house of the LORD, because the glory of the LORD had filled the LORD's house." (2 Chron. 7:1,2) That is the former glory. The latter glory is greater!

When GOD truly dwells in His church we arrive at where He wants us to be and the power available becomes phenomenal which we will now look at in more detail.

Power over all sickness and disease

Jesus went around healing people and raising the dead and doing incredible miracles. Anyone who reads the scriptures will be fully aware of the wonder of some of these miracles. But Jesus didn't keep the power to himself. We are told "Jesus called his twelve disciples to him and gave them authority to drive out impure spirits and to heal every disease and sickness. ... These twelve Jesus sent out with the following instructions...As you go, proclaim this message: 'The kingdom of heaven has come near.' Heal the sick, raise the dead, cleanse those who have leprosy, drive out demons. Freely you have received; freely give." (Mt 10:1f.)

But then it wasn't only for the 12 either. Luke tells us "After this the Lord appointed seventy-two others and sent them two by two ahead of him to every town and place where he was about to go." We are then told "the seventy-two returned with joy and said, "Lord, even the demons submit to us in your name." He replied, "I saw Satan fall like lightning from heaven. I have given you authority to trample on snakes and scorpions and to overcome all the power of the enemy; nothing will harm you." (Luke 10:1,17-19). They had authority over sickness going out at Jesus's command together.

But then Jesus says the most amazing thing to his disciples in the upper room, "truly I tell you, whoever believes in me will do the works I have been doing, and they will do even greater things than these, because I am going to the Father. And I will do whatever you ask in my name, so that the Father may be glorified in the Son. You may ask me for anything in my name, and I will do it." Jesus says there is absolutely no limit to what you will be able to do. This is so amazing it pays us to stop a minute and think about this. After the church received the outpouring of the Holy Spirit on the Day of Pentecost we got a glimpse of it in Acts 5:15,16 "As a result, people brought the sick into the streets and laid them on beds and mats so that at least Peter's shadow might fall on some of them as he passed by. Crowds gathered also from the towns around Jerusalem, bringing their sick and those tormented by impure spirits, and all of them were healed." Or Acts 19:11,12 "God did extraordinary miracles through Paul, so that even handkerchiefs and aprons that had touched him were taken to the sick, and their illnesses were cured and the evil spirits left them." These were miracles Jesus never did but were absolutely extraordinary. We are not yet beginning to move in half the power God has given to His church. What is stopping us taking this power into the political realm? There is nothing that Jesus taught that is stopping us.

Glory

Matthew 17 says "After six days Jesus took with him Peter, James and John the brother of James, and led them up a high mountain by themselves. There he was transfigured before them. His face shone like the sun, and his clothes became as white as the light. Just then there appeared before them Moses and Elijah, talking with Jesus. ... While he was still speaking, a bright cloud covered them, and a voice from the cloud said, "This is my Son, whom I love; with him I am well pleased. Listen to him!" When the disciples heard this, they fell facedown to the ground, terrified." Peter and John were with Jesus. John when he wrote said, "The Word became flesh and made his dwelling among us. We have seen his glory, the glory of the one and only Son, who came from the Father, full of grace and truth." (Jn 1:14) John said we saw His glory. Peter when he was writing said, "we did not follow cleverly devised stories when we told you about the coming of our Lord Jesus Christ in power, but we were eyewitnesses of his majesty. He received honour and glory from God the Father when the voice came to him from the Majestic Glory, saying, "This is my Son, whom I love; with him I am well pleased." We ourselves heard this voice that came from heaven when we were with him on the sacred mountain." (2 Peter 1:16-18). It was a staggering experience that left a deep impact on those who saw it.

Amazingly though Jesus says, "you can experience that". When he prays in John 17 he prays first for his disciples then he prays for "those who will believe in me through their word." That's us. He then says, "I have given them the glory that you gave me." (Jn17:22) But the context is unity in the body, "that they may be one". So this is about the church.

In 2 Chron. 5 we read of all the people worshipping and coming to the newly built temple. It then says, "it happened, when the trumpet players and singers made one sound to praise and give thanks to the Lord, and when they lifted up their voice with the trumpets and cymbals and all the instruments of music and praised the Lord saying, "For He is good and His mercy endures forever," that the house, the house of the Lord, was filled with a cloud. And the priests were not able to stand in order to serve because of the cloud, for the glory of the Lord had filled the house of God." (2 Chronicles 5:13-14).

Moses also experienced the glory of God, but he experienced it as a representative of the people. "When Moses came down from Mount Sinai with the two tablets of the covenant law in his hands, he was not aware that his face was radiant because he had spoken with the Lord. "When Aaron and all the Israelites saw Moses, his face was radiant, and they were afraid to come near him. But Moses called to them; so Aaron and all the leaders of the community came back to him, and he spoke to them. Afterward all the Israelites came near him, and he gave them all the commands the Lord had given him on Mount Sinai. When Moses finished speaking to them, he put a veil over his face." (Exodus 34:29-33). This was their leader, leading the people into a closer relationship with their Lord.

Acts 6 said the church chose Stephen for a specific task. "They chose Stephen, a man full of faith and the Holy Spirit... and Stephen, full of faith and power, did great wonders and signs among the people. Then there arose some from what is called the Synagogue of the Freedmen (Cyrenians, Alexandrians, and those from Cilicia and Asia), disputing with Stephen. And they were not able to resist the wisdom and the Spirit by which he spoke. Then they secretly induced men to say, "We have heard him speak blasphemous words against Moses and God." And they stirred up the people, the elders, and the scribes; and they came upon *him,* seized him, and brought *him* to the council...and all who sat in the council, looking steadfastly at him, saw his face as the face of an angel." Stephen experienced the glory as a man chosen by the church to represent them.

The glory of God is not meant to be imparted to a few believers on their own. It is meant to be imparted to the church acting in unison, or representatives of the church speaking out as God has called them to speak out.

Authority over the Nations

This is now the context in which we then move on to see Jesus saying that He has authority over the nations, which we looked at, at the beginning of the introduction. This authority He also gives it to us and we can also walk in authority over the nations as a unified pure holy praycrful church that does not tolerate sexual immorality.

There is one more point of note here. Joshua had a tremendous victory over Jericho because he listened to God and got His strategy which sounded foolish but by obeying what sounded a foolish instruction (walk round the walls once a day for 6 days and then on the 7th day walk round 7 times) the walls fell down. Full of confidence in that victory he sent a small army to Ai without asking God. They were defeated the reason being because one man had sinned. Achan had taken some gold from Jericho and dug a hole and hidden it in his tent. It turned out he "saw among the spoils a beautiful Babylonian garment, two hundred shekels of silver, and a wedge of gold weighing fifty shekels, coveted them and took them". God said "*There is* an accursed thing in your midst, O Israel; you cannot stand before your enemies until you take away the accursed thing from among you." (Joshua 7:13). One man had sinned but God allowed the nation to suffer defeat because of the sin of that one man. That sin had to be exposed before Israel could have victory. It was exposed and dealt with and Israel had victory again.

The release of power as a result of purity was not only Ai being defeated. Very soon we read, "So Joshua conquered all the land: the mountain country and the South and the lowland and the wilderness slopes, and all their kings; he left none remaining, but utterly destroyed all that breathed, as the Lord God of Israel had commanded. And Joshua conquered them from Kadesh Barnea as far as Gaza, and all the country of Goshen, even as far as Gibeon. All these kings and their land Joshua took at one time, because the Lord God of Israel fought for Israel." (Joshua 10:40-42) He never faced defeat again having dealt with the sin.

The early church moved in incredible power after the Holy Spirit came and the apostles were able to stand in front of the Sanhedrin and defy them because God was with them. They also cared for each other in such a way that "the multitude of those who believed were of one heart and one soul; neither did anyone say that any of the things he possessed was his own, but they had all things in common. And with great power the apostles gave witness to the resurrection of the Lord Jesus. And great grace was upon them all. Nor was there anyone among them who lacked; for all who were possessors of lands or houses sold them, and brought the proceeds of the things that were sold, and laid *them* at the apostles' feet; and they distributed to each as anyone had need." (Acts 4:32-35) But there was a problem. Peter was in tune with the Holy Spirit and something was revealed to him. "Ananias, why has Satan filled your heart to lie to the Holy Spirit and keep back *part* of the price of the land for yourself? While it remained, was it not your own? And after it was sold, was it not in your own control? Why have you conceived this thing in your heart? You have not lied to men but to God." (Acts 5:3,4)

Ananias and his wife dropped down dead and then came the release of power as sin was dealt with and multitudes believed. The result was "great fear came upon all the church and upon all who heard these things. And through the hands of the apostles many signs and wonders were done among the people. And they were all with one accord in Solomon's Porch... the people esteemed them highly and believers were increasingly added to the Lord, multitudes of both men and women" (Acts 5:11-14). God was not willing to tolerate any sin in Israel and he wasn't willing to tolerate any sin in his church. However, when His people listened to Him and acted the result was not a return to normal. Incredible power was released, far more than before.

This is the message of 1 Corinthians 5 looked at later. Now let's be clear about this. We are not meant to go around judging people. We are however meant to seek total purity within the body of Christ as a condition of being able to take authority in His name over nations. Church leaders have to deal with sin in the church or be weak and useless. In the examples quoted above it was God who revealed the sin and His servants then dealt with it. We have to be in that place where we will not tolerate any sin among God's people and allow Him to reveal what He wants to reveal and if He reveals something, we have to deal with it. That is the condition for God's authority in Government. To the extent that this is not done now is the extent to which God's people are weak and Satan's agenda is gaining in the nation. We cannot cut corners. If we tolerate sin, we have no spiritual authority, simple as that. If we don't tolerate it, we can have authority over nations."

Does this mean we are seeking to bring about God's kingdom through politics? No. Jesus is very clear "my kingdom is not from the world". We don't only have authority because we win an election. We have authority from God. However, if the whole nation is united in seeking the will of God and elects a Christian Government that is operating correctly under the authority of God then certainly that is a springboard for authority in the realm of healing and for release of the glory of God. It is not an end, but it is a means to an end.

There is no reason at all why we should not have a Prime Minister full of the Holy Ghost with his or her face shining with the glory standing at the despatch box in the House of Commons and MPs supporting him or her dedicated to doing and obeying the will of God. Do you think this just might be a trigger for revival in the nation? There is no short cut. Either we have revival on God's terms or we don't have it. God will never give revival to a weak compromised church.

The context in which God calls his church to operate is from receiving power and authority because of purity and obedience. But now let's look at the foundation upon which we are told to build. The church has to be prepared to take power having first got the foundation in place.

The foundation

We are told that the church where God's Spirit dwells is built on the foundation of the apostles and prophets. What does that look like?

Many churches are focussed almost entirely on pastors caring for the flock. Good pastors then become bishops who are caring for the pastors. The favoured bishop then becomes an archbishop caring for the bishops. When someone stands up in church and says "I believe God is saying..." often they are unwelcome. Why? Because they may well be challenging and causing stress to the happy flock of sheep being carefully pastored. It is not that pastors and teachers are not needed in the church. Absolutely they are but as we shall see in a later chapter if all we have in the church is pastoral care then truth, righteousness and holiness can easily be discarded.

But God is not finished with His church. Increasingly in modern times groups of apostles and prophets have sprung up apart from any one recognised church but gathering together in their own group. One such group Sid has been involved with is called the Inter Prophetic and Apostolic

Alliance. The main feature of this group is a passionate desire to hear what God is saying, to honour it and flow in it. Jesus said, "My sheep hear my voice and I know them and they follow me" (John 10:27). The prophet spends all his or her time listening to God and then communicates what they hear to the apostle who puts it into practice with lots of new initiatives driving the church forward.

Now at this point we need a word of caution. Jesus said "When he has brought out all his own, he goes on ahead of them, and his sheep follow him because they know his voice. But they will never follow a stranger; in fact, they will run away from him because they do not recognize a stranger's voice." (John10:4,5) That tells us that there are also strangers speaking. Because we are human beings and fallible, we can make mistakes so we have to speak humbly and say "I believe God is saying..." and allow others to test the word. No Christian should ever take the position "God has spoken to me. If you argue with me you are arguing with God." That is arrogant and very dangerous. In fact, this is one way heresies have crept into the church, by people thinking they have heard from God and speaking it out and refusing any correction.

Paul tells us "The spirits of prophets are subject to the control of prophets. For God is not a God of disorder but of peace — as in all the congregations of the Lord's people." (1

Cor 14:32,33) Again he says, "Do not treat prophecies with contempt but test them all; hold on to what is good, reject every kind of evil." (1 Thess. 5:20-22). Because sometimes all prophets make mistakes and get things wrong that is not a reason to reject prophecy. Our position has to be that we are earnestly seeking the will of God and seeking to hear what He has to say. We will always keep earnestly seeking to hear. God calls us to that relationship with him described most beautifully in Rev 3:20, "Here I am! I stand at the door and knock. If anyone hears my voice and opens the door, I will come in and eat with that person, and they with me." Note it is hearing His voice that leads us to open the door and sit down and share time together. We talk to Him and He talks to us and we get to know each other. We get to know each other's heart and each other's desire. The more time we spend in His presence the less likely we are to make a mistake.

Now this foundation is in place we can go onto talk more about politics. If we can hear God's voice and we believe that He is interested in absolutely everything that goes on in the world then we can find out His will in any and every situation. We can say "God what is your heart over the European Union?" and listen to the answer. We can say "God what is your heart over nuclear weapons?" and listen to the answer. We can say "God what is your heart over Syria?" and listen to the answer. We can say "God what sort of tax policy do you want us to have?" and listen to the answer. This is how the Christian Peoples Alliance manifesto was developed which is outlined in detail in Chapter 6. The aim is not just to develop a manifesto all Christians can support but to develop a manifesto that the whole world can see is the best answer to every problem. If we are able to tap into the fount of all knowledge, then we should have the best manifesto by far and it should be possible for the whole world to recognise it and want to vote for it. That is our vision. This is wisdom from above and it is "first of all pure; then peace-loving, considerate, submissive, full of mercy and good fruit, impartial and sincere. Peacemakers who sow in peace reap a harvest of righteousness." (James 3:17,18). Moreover, it is a gift that God has given to His church. "The manifestation of the Spirit is given to each one for the profit of all. For to one is give the word of wisdom through the Spirit." (I Cor 12:7,18). We need that word of wisdom operating in the political realm more than any other.

So, what is stopping us moving now into the realm of politics and taking over? The answer is that any Christian involvement in politics will come against a very powerful Satanic agenda that hates everything we stand for. As has already been shown a united body of Christ can take authority over this agenda and destroy it, but in order to defeat it we first have to know exactly what it is and why it is wrong. This is what we will look at in the next chapter. The extent to which we are not currently united and moving in the authority God has given us is the extent to which this agenda is being implemented and the extent we need to do something about it. The fact is at the moment the church is not victorious over the Satanic agenda. We will now look at what it is and therefore what we need to defeat and why.

CHAPTER 3
Facing the Satanic Agenda

"You have enemies? Good. That means you've stood up for something, sometime in your life"

Winston Churchill

John wrote "And the Word became flesh and dwelt among us, and we have seen his glory, glory as of the only Son from the Father, full of grace and truth." (Jn 1:14). When looking at this chapter we urge the reader to consider that Jesus stood for both grace and truth. Grace is repentance and forgiveness. Truth is holiness and righteousness and God's law and His nature. If a church has all grace and no truth, then it offers forgiveness to everyone but never talks about sin or holiness or Gods standard and so easily accepts things in the church God calls sin. If a church has all truth and no grace it is hard and uncompromising and preaches hell and damnation without offering love, repentance and forgiveness. When studying this chapter please bear in mind the church that is walking in God's plans and purposes has to operate in both together. When people fail, we don't condemn them. We offer them redemption, but that does not alter God's standard one iota.

Two other references are important before we go into the detail. In Mt 10:27 Jesus said, "What I tell you in the dark, speak in the daylight; what is whispered in your ear, proclaim from the roofs." In Luke 8:17 Jesus said, "there is nothing hidden that will not be disclosed, and nothing concealed that will not be known or brought out into the open". In bringing this agenda into the light and exposing it for what it is we are doing something God calls us to do. So long as it remains hidden, we are left confused as to what is going on and where it is coming from. When we know where it is coming from we can defeat and destroy it.

The two kingdoms, deceit and truth

Jesus said to the Pharisees "You belong to your father, the devil, and you want to carry out your father's desires. He was a murderer from the beginning, not holding to the truth, for there is no truth in him. When he lies, he speaks his native language, for he is a liar and the father of lies. Yet because I tell the truth, you do not believe me! Can any of you prove me guilty of sin? If I am telling the truth, why don't you believe me? Whoever belongs to God hears what God says. The reason you do not hear is that you do not belong to God."

There are two kingdoms. Satan's kingdom ruled over by lies and God's kingdom ruled over by the truth. Jesus said "I am the truth". When we tell lies we align ourselves with Satan. When we tell the truth we align ourselves with God. To be effective as ambassadors for God in politics we have to be 100% devoted to telling the truth at all times no matter what the repercussions and also to expose lies. This is very important because one of the features of politics is deceitful language. A common expression is "he spoke that like a politician" which usually means what he said wasn't totally untrue, but he was concealing something when he said it. As Christians in politics we must not conform to that way of speaking, but boldly declare what is true at all times even if it is hard to do so. (John 8:44-47)

We will now look at Satan's agenda and expose what he is after.

Helena Blavatsky 1831 to 1891 is the founder of the Theosophical Society which is study of the occult. She was also the first person to talk about the New Age. Her writings are extensive and full of all sorts of Satanic content. Of greater interest to us however is Alice Bailey. She lived 1880 to 1949 and wrote 24 books. She became president of the Theosophical Society established by Helena Blavatsky. She also established the Lucis Trust Goodwill (to which is linked the leadership of the World Constitution and Parliament Association) under the name Lucifer Publishing Company which today boasts of a membership of more than 6000 people. Some of the world's most renowned financial and political leaders have belonged to this organization.

The New Age Movement.

Its main goal is to destroy traditional Judeo Christianity and create a one world Religion based on a Luciferian system and doctrine. Let us Explore the foundations of that which Governs this Nation and how the adversary and his plan to indoctrinate society into rebelling against God's Laws.

These are the four Pillars of the New Age Movement

Evolution. Claiming evolution explains the origins of life is denying God as creator of the world a concept central to Christianity and something proclaimed round the throne of God, (Revelation 4:11)

Reincarnation. This is denying heaven and hell something clearly taught by Jesus. E.g. for heaven John 14:1-6 For hell e.g. Matthew 10:28.

Astrology. This is denying the plans and purposes of God for His children and promotes the idea that everything is decided in advance by fate.

Meditation. This takes the place of prayer and is designed so people open themselves up to the demonic realm to be taken over by demons rather than opening themselves to the Spirit of God and for His Holy Spirit to possess them.

Alice Bailey put forward a 10-point charter which is placed in the House of Lords and House of Commons in our

Parliament. Today our governments and many politicians are implementing the strategy. How we need to replace it with the strategy of heaven. We will go over it point by point quoting what Alice Bailey says. In order to show how each point is directly contrary to God's plan and purposes, scriptures have then quoted briefly against each point.

1. TAKE GOD AND PRAYER OUT OF THE EDUCATION SYSTEM

Alice Bailey wrote that the curriculum should be changed to ensure that children are freed from the bondage of Christian culture. Why? Because children go to school to be equipped to face life, they are willing to trust and they are willing to value what is being given to them. If you take God out of education, they will unconsciously form a resolve that God is not necessary to face life. She also said encourage children to engage in transcendental meditation which opens their minds to the occult.

Children are very important to God

Whoever receives one such child in my name receives me, but whoever causes one of these little ones who believe in me to sin, it would be better for him to have a great millstone fastened round his neck and to be drowned in the depth of the sea. (Mt 18:5,6)

Then children were brought to him that he might lay his hands on them and pray. The disciples rebuked the people, but Jesus said, "Let the little children come to me and do not hinder them, for to such belongs the kingdom of heaven." (Mt 19:13,14)

2. REDUCE PARENTAL AUTHORITY OVER THE CHILDREN

Break the communication between parent and child so that parents do not pass on their Christian traditions to their children, liberate children from the bondage of their parental traditions.
a)Promote excessive child rights
b) Abolish corporal punishment
c) Teachers are the agents of implementation.

The Child Parent Relationship is very important to God
Train up a child in the way he should go; even when he is old he will not depart from it. (Proverbs 22:6)
Children, obey your parents in the Lord, for this is right. (Eph 6:1)
"Honour your father and your mother, that your days may be long in the land that the Lord your God is giving you.(Ex 20:12)Anyone who curses his father or his mother shall surely be put to death; (Lev 20:9)

By contrast Jesus predicted under Satanic rebellion "children will rise against parents and have them put to death" (Mt 10:21) Paul said "people will be disobedient to their parents..." (1 Tim 3:2)

3. DESTROY THE JUDEO-CHRISTIAN FAMILY STRUCTURE

a) Promote sexual promiscuity – Free young people to the concept of premarital sex, let them have free sex, lift it so high that the joy of enjoying it is the highest joy in life, fantasize it, that everybody will feel proud to be seen to be sexually active, even those outside of marriage.

b)Use advertising industry, media – T.V., magazines, film industry to promote sexual enjoyment as the highest pleasure in humanity.

Sexual purity is taught throughout the Bible
God says, also quoted by Jesus, "Therefore a man shall leave his father and his mother and hold fast to his wife, and they shall become one flesh." (Gen 2:24, Mt 19) Paul says "… But fornication and all uncleanness or covetousness, let it not even be named among you, as is fitting for saints… for this you know, that no fornicator, unclean person, nor covetous man, who is an idolater has any inheritance in the kingdom of Christ and God." (Eph 5:3-5)

4. IF SEX IS FREE, THEN MAKE ABORTION LEGAL AND MAKE IT EASY

She said; "Build clinics for abortion – Health clinics in schools"

'Abortion as told by Christians is oppressive and denies our rights, we have a right to choose whether we want to have a child or not. If a woman does not want the pregnancy, she should have the freedom to get rid of that pregnancy as painlessly and as easily as possible'.

God forms life in the mother's womb

Before I formed you in the womb I knew you, and before you were born I consecrated you (Jer 1:5)

For you formed my inward parts; you knitted me together in my mother's womb. I praise you, for I am fearfully and wonderfully made. (Ps 139:13,14). If God forms you in your mother's womb you cannot kill what God has formed.

The Lord spoke to Moses, saying, "Say to the people of Israel, Any one of the people of Israel or of the strangers who sojourn in Israel who gives any of his children to Molech shall surely be put to death." (Lev 20:1,2) This is child sacrifice railed against in Leviticus 20 which abortion is a form of.

5. MAKE DIVORCE EASY AND LEGAL

FREE PEOPLE FROM THE CONCEPT OF MARRIAGE FOR LIFE. She said "don't be held in bondage by the Christian values it will never come back, what you need is an easily arranged divorce and allow another love bond to come forth, just like an ovum comes up, and when it comes forth you'll enjoy life again. "

God Hates Divorce
"...the Lord was witness between you and the wife of your youth, to whom you have been faithless, though she is your companion and your wife by covenant. Did he not make them one, with a portion of the Spirit in their union? And what was the one God seeking? Godly offspring. So guard yourselves in your spirit, and let none of you be faithless to the wife of your youth. Indeed, the Lord God of Israel says that he hates divorce. So guard yourselves in your spirit, and do not be faithless." (Mal 2:14-16) The primary reason for faithfulness in marriage is to provide a secure environment for children to be brought into the world with a mother and father who will love and care for them all their life.

6. MAKE HOMOSEXUALITY AN ALTERNATIVE LIFESTYLE

Alice Bailey preached that sexual enjoyment is the highest pleasure in humanity, no one must be denied and no one must be restricted how to enjoy themselves. People should be allowed, in whichever way they chose to do what they want, whether it is homosexuality or incest or bestiality, as long as the two agree.

Jesus taught sexual purity

Jesus answered, "Have you not read that he who created them from the beginning made them male and female, and said, 'Therefore a man shall leave his father and his mother and hold fast to his wife..." (Mt 19:4,5) There is no possibility here of two men or two women being married. Jesus is very clear God made man and woman to come together in marriage. This is the same theme Paul expands on in Rom 1:18f. Creation tells us what is right.

Jesus said "what comes out of the mouth proceeds from the heart, and this defiles a person. For out of the heart come evil thoughts, murder, adultery, sexual immorality, theft, false witness, slander. These are what defile a person." (Mt15:19) The Greek for "sexual immorality" is "porneia". The meaning of porneia is described in full here http://moleski.net/cac/Porneia. It includes all sex gay or straight outside of marriage between a man and a woman.

Then Jesus said, "Do not think that I have come to abolish the Law or the Prophets; I have not come to abolish them but to fulfil them...." (Mt 5:17)."Do not have sexual relations with a man as one does with a woman; that is detestable." "If a man has sexual relations with a man as one does with a woman, both of them have done what is detestable. They are to be put to death; their blood will be on their own heads." (Lev 18:22, 20:13) Now we don't put people to death because we believe Jesus has born the punishment of the law for us so all who repent are forgiven but the standard has not changed.

We also know that Paul is referring to these verses when he says, "Or do you not know that wrongdoers will not inherit the kingdom of God? Do not be deceived: Neither the sexually immoral nor idolaters nor adulterers nor men who have sex with men ἄρσενος κοίτην. (arsenokoitein) ... will inherit the kingdom of God. And that is what some of you were. But you were washed, you were sanctified, you were justified in the name of the Lord Jesus Christ and by the Spirit of our God." (1Cor 6:9,10) The only time the word ἄρσενος κοίτην (arsenokoitein)appears in the Old Testament, in the Greek translation of the Hebrew original called the Septuagint (LXX), is Lev 18:22 and Lev 20:13. We know Paul had this as he quoted from it word for word.

The truth is that every sort of homosexuality is condemned in the Bible.

7. DEBASE ART, MAKE IT RUN MAD

Promote new forms of art which will corrupt and defile the imagination of people because art is the language of the spirit, that which is inside, you can bring out in painting, music, drama etc. Look at the quality of the music that is coming out and types of films out of Hollywood, even comedy episodes promote a lot of immoral behaviour, children shows, the list goes on.

Praise and worship is central to faith

Jesus said "The hour is coming, and is now here, when the true worshippers will worship the Father in spirit and truth, for the Father is seeking such people to worship him God is spirit, and those who worship him must worship in spirit and truth (John 4:23,24)

"...he said with a loud voice, "Fear God and give him glory, because the hour of his judgement has come, and worship him who made heaven and earth, the sea and the springs of water."... And another angel, a third, followed them, saying with a loud voice, "If anyone worships the beast and its image and receives a mark on his forehead or on his hand, he also will drink the wine of God's wrath, poured full strength into the cup of his anger, and he will be tormented with fire and sulphur in the presence of the holy angels and in the presence of the Lamb. " (Rev 14:7-10)

8. USE MEDIA TO PROMOTE AND CHANGE MINDSET

Alice Bailey said the greatest channel you need to use to change human attitude is media. Use the press, the radio, TV, cinema. So much money is pumped into media and advertising to spread pornographic material and other sources. Sex outside of marriage is thrown in your face 80-90 times a day rather than sex in marriage. Promiscuity is being promoted as natural. Gay sex is being shown on TV conditioning people to accept their New Age Agendas.

Our Minds Are key
"If then you have been raised with Christ, seek the things that are above, where Christ is, seated at the right hand of God. Set your minds on things that are above, not on things that are on earth. For you have died, and your life is hidden with Christ in God. When Christ who is your life appears, then you also will appear with him in glory.
Put to death therefore what is earthly in you: sexual immorality, impurity, passion, evil desire, and covetousness, which is idolatry. On account of these the wrath of God is coming. In these you too once walked, when

you were living in them. But now you must put them all away." (Col 3:1-5)

9. **CREATE AN INTERFAITH MOVEMENT**

Alice Bailey wrote; Promote other faiths to be at par with Christianity and break this thing about Christianity as being the only way to heaven, by that Christianity will be pulled down and other faiths promoted. She said promote the importance of man in determining his own future and destiny – **HUMANISM.** She said tell man he has the right to choose what he wants to be, and he can make it happen, he has the right to determine his cause – This takes God off His throne.

There are many other faiths promoted alongside Christianity but the one that seems to have gained the most traction is Islam.

How Christianity and Islam are Incompatible
The Qur'an says Jesus did not die on the cross (4;157) Jesus's death is the means of salvation for a Christian.
The Qur'an says that if you say Jesus was the son of God you will go to hell (5:72). Jesus's divinity is central to Christianity.

The Qur'an says before Allah you can only be a slave (19:93). Jesus says he wants to be our friend and wants to have a relationship with us.

Islam tells you to say the same prayer 5 times a day. Jesus said not to do this "for they think they will be heard for their many words" but to pray simply and specifically.

The Qur'an says to kill disbelievers (9:5) and cut off their heads (47:4). Jesus says to love your enemies and do good to those who hate you.

The Qur'an says Allah is the best of deceivers (3:54,8:30) Jesus claimed to be the truth and said the truth will set you free. He also said he was the only way to the father. There is not more than one way.

We could equally show how every other faith is also incompatible with Christianity but the differences with Islam are perhaps less understood.

10.   GET GOVERNMENTS TO MAKE ALL THESE LAWS AND GET THE CHURCH TO ENDORSE THESE CHANGES.

Alice Bailey wrote that the church must change its doctrine and accommodate the people by accepting these things and put them into its structures and systems. The New Age Movement's ultimate goal is to establish a One World Government, a One World Economic system and a One World Religion. Today the strategy almost in its entirety has been adopted by the United Nations and today a lot of it is already law in many nations. This deception has crept up unobserved on so many people.

God wants His church to be pure and Holy

I wrote to you in my letter not to associate with sexually immoral people — not at all meaning the sexually immoral of this world, or the greedy and swindlers, or idolaters, since then you would need to go out of the world. But now I am writing to you not to associate with anyone who bears the name of brother if he is guilty of sexual immorality or greed, or is an idolater, reviler, drunkard, or swindler — not even to eat with such a one. For what have I to do with judging outsiders? Is it not those inside the church whom you are to judge? God judges[b] those outside. "Purge the evil person from among you." (1 Cor 5:9-13)

CHAPTER 4
The State of the Church in the UK

"Accustom yourself to look first to the dreadful consequences of failure; then fix your eye on the glorious prize which is before you; and when your strength begins to fail, and your spirits are well nigh exhausted, let the animating view rekindle your resolution, and call forth in renewed vigour the fainting energies of your soul."

William Wilberforce

Point 10 of the agenda we looked at in the last chapter is to "get the church to endorse these changes". So the Satanic agenda is to corrupt and take control of the church of God. How successful are they being?

The church is very important to God. It is not only where He dwells as we saw from Ephesians 2 it is also His body. As we saw at the end of Chapter one God demands total purity before He will do anything through His church. That's why many Biblical statements are so brutal but we need to look at them.

God's heart is holiness, purity, righteousness. 1 Peter 1:13-16 has an order for the church to be holy. "Therefore gird up the loins of your mind, be sober, and rest your hope fully upon the grace that is to be brought to you at the revelation of Jesus Christ; as obedient children, not conforming yourselves to the former lusts, as in your ignorance; but as He who called you is holy, you also be holy in all your conduct, because it is written, "Be holy, for I am holy."
Eph 6:14 says we have to put on the "Breastplate of righteousness". It is essential for protection of our hearts and bodies.
Ps 89:14, 97:2 say "Justice and Righteousness are the foundation of His throne" They are both principles on which God's throne is built and are fundamental to who He is.

Rev 4:8 says round the throne there is a sound constantly,
"Holy, holy, holy,
Lord God Almighty, Who was and is and is to come!"

This is the sound of heaven. Some would prefer they were crying "Loving, loving, loving, is the Lord God Almighty." God is loving, but we only experience His love when we repent. The father always loved the prodigal son but when he was in a far country engaging in riotous living he didn't experience the father's love. He only experienced that love when he came back and repented of his sin. So with us.

So, we come back to Paul. We quote 1 Cor 5 again more fully. "It is actually reported that there is sexual immorality among you, and of a kind that even pagans do not tolerate: A man is sleeping with his father's wife. And you are proud! Shouldn't you rather have gone into mourning and have put out of your fellowship the man who has been doing this? For my part, even though I am not physically present, I am with you in spirit. As one who is present with you in this way, I have already passed judgment in the name of our Lord Jesus on the one who has been doing this. So when you are assembled and I am with you in spirit, and the power of our Lord Jesus is present, hand this man over to Satan for the destruction of the flesh, so that his spirit may be saved on the day of the Lord. ... I wrote to you in my letter not to associate with sexually immoral people – not at all meaning the people of this world who are immoral, or the greedy and swindlers, or idolaters. In that case you would have to leave this world. But now I am writing to you that you must not associate with anyone who claims to be a brother or sister but is sexually immoral or greedy, an idolater or slanderer, a drunkard or swindler. Do not even eat with such people. What business is it of mine to judge those outside the church? Are you not to judge those inside? God will judge those outside. "Expel the wicked person from among you."

That's God's standard holiness. How does the church stack up?

Churches in the UK that tolerate homosexuality: -

United Kingdom (UK) - Church of England

The church has a mixed position. The church defines marriage as between a man and a woman, but also supports same-sex civil partnerships.

The church says it "supports clergy who are in civil partnerships." The church allows transgender priests. The C of E allows prayers to follow a civil same-sex marriage, and allows civil partnerships for gay priests. In 2016, the Bishop of Grantham came out as the first openly gay bishop in a relationship. When they say they are celibate that is highly questionable. How can Jeffrey John, Dean of St Albans be celibate when he's in a civil partnership and wants to have a same sex marriage?

The result is as follows: - Guardian headline Sept 2018 "Church in crisis as only 2% of young adults identify as C of E" That is under 24s. The article also says, "The proportion of people of all ages identifying with the C of E has fallen from 31% in 2002 to 14% last year."

There are signs that Justin Welby might be moving back to supporting Orthodox Christianity. There has been a terrible period where he described same sex marriage as "great" and apologised to the US church for the hurt caused to them by being excluded from the Anglican family for supporting same sex marriage.

He has encouraged the teaching of transsexualism in C of E schools. In response GAFCON has been set up to stand for Orthodox Christianity. Justin Welby has set the next once in a decade Lambeth Conference as Thursday 23 July until Sunday 2 August 2020. The Archbishops of Uganda, Nigeria, Rwanda and most of the bishops from South America have made it clear they will not attend unless the church returns to Biblical values.

Now Justin Welby has responded by saying "whatever views we come with, we come to be under the authority of Scripture, and inspired by the Spirit." The theme of the

Conference will be 1 Peter. Peter talks a lot about sinful desires and holiness. "As obedient children, do not conform to the evil desires you had when you lived in ignorance. But just as he who called you is holy, so be holy in all you do; for it is written: "Be holy, because I am holy." (1 Peter 1:14-16). Then Dear friends, I urge you, as foreigners and exiles, to abstain from sinful desires, which wage war against your soul. (1 Peter 2:13) "you have spent enough time in the past doing what pagans choose to do—living in debauchery, lust, drunkenness, orgies, carousing and detestable idolatry.... but live according to God in regard to the spirit." (1 Peter 4:3,6) If Justin Welby is serious about being under the authority of Scripture and is following 1 Peter then he will be forced to condemn homosexuality and transsexualism and assisted dying and Islam. It will be a dramatic change in his stance. We hope he is serious but wait to see. He has said he sees climate change in 1 Peter so there is a concern he will see what he wants to see not what the text says. If Justin Welby brings the C of E back to Orthodox Christianity, we will be thrilled. If he is trying to deceive us about being under the authority of Scripture, then judgement on the C of E will be the greater.

UK - Church in Wales:

A majority supports same-sex marriage; the church said LGBT people can be "honest and open, respected and affirmed" which presumably means affirmed as homosexuals and not encouraged to change in any way. The church also permits gay priests to enter into civil partnerships. Less than 1% of the people of Wales go to the Church in Wales.

It's web site says, "The Church in Wales believes and proclaims the Good News of Jesus Christ, namely:
*that God is active and personal, a Father who cares for his creation, and for every human being as his beloved child;
*that God is as he has revealed himself to be in the historical person of Jesus Christ, and
*that through the life, death and resurrection of this one person, God has proclaimed his love for the world, and opened a way, accessible through our response of faith, by which his love and life may be poured into our lives.
*That God is at work in the world today as Spirit, inspiring faith, justice and truth.
We believe that God has called all who respond to him to be his people, and to work together to act as ambassadors for his work of healing in the world.
This is Good News, because it encourages each one of us to realise that God loves us, that he has gone out of his way to meet us in the person of his Son, in whom he accepts us as we are. He asks us to draw on his strength to live life to the full, and to bring healing to the world. We invite you to join with us in sharing this Good News."

On the face of it this may appear good, but a closer examination shows there is no mention of holiness or righteousness or of repentance and forgiveness. The statement says God "accepts us as we are" which is true but He doesn't leave us as we are. He invites us to repent and be born again into a new and living hope. Sadly, it would appear that for the Church in Wales "accepts us as we are" means accepts sin which is totally wrong.

UK - Scottish Episcopal Church

In June 2017 the Scottish Episcopal Church voted to allow gay couples to marry in church making it the first major Christian church in the UK to allow same-sex marriages. It's web site also says it has a proud record of engagement in interfaith relations in Scotland." Its membership is declining fast to currently around half of 1% of the people who live in Scotland.

On its web site the Scottish Episcopal church asks, "What is Christianity?" It starts by quoting 1 John 4:16 "God is love, and those who live in love live in God, and God lives in them". It continues "Jesus taught and lived a life of loving God and loving our neighbour. He was deeply concerned with the inequity of wealth, where some starved and some lived in luxury. He challenged unjust systems in his own society, basing his ministry of healing and preaching on compassion for the poor and those who were shunned by society, such as lepers, prostitutes, people of other religions, criminals, the "unclean". As so often happens to those who speak truth to power, the Roman rulers and the Jewish religious leaders were determined to silence him, and Jesus was crucified."

Though most of the above is correct the reason why Jesus was crucified was because he claimed to be God. "The high priest said to him, "I charge you under oath by the living God: Tell us if you are the Messiah, the Son of God." "You have said so," Jesus replied. "But I say to all of you: from now on you will see the Son of Man sitting at the right hand of the Mighty One and coming on the clouds of heaven." Then the high priest tore his clothes and said, "He has spoken blasphemy! Why do we need any more witnesses? Look, now you have heard the blasphemy. What do you think?" "He is worthy of death," they answered." (Mt 26:63-66) For a church to get this wrong is quite basic.

Again, in all their writings there is no mention of holiness or righteousness or repentance and forgiveness. Without repentance this church is not preaching the gospel. But in a sense what they have done is worse. They have actually made up their own reason for Jesus's crucifixion which is not historical, but which is what they would have liked it to be. It is highly misleading and since Jesus's crucifixion is fundamental to Christianity places this church in an invidious position.

UK - Methodist Church of Great Britain

The church may bless civil same-sex marriages. Methodists have seen a decline of approximately one third in their total membership in the past 10 years.

Their web site says, "The calling of the Methodist Church is:
To increase awareness of God's presence and to celebrate God's love.
To help people to grow and learn as Christians, through mutual support and care.
To be a good neighbour to people in need and to challenge injustice.
To make more followers of Jesus Christ."

They then go onto say "As we begin to engage in relations with people of other faiths, we find that our awareness of God at work in others' lives is sharpened.... Through explaining our beliefs to others and being open to the responses of those from other faiths, we gain a greater insight into the truth of the God we worship through Jesus Christ." We examined under point 9 of the Satanic Agenda why Islam and Christianity are incompatible. It appears that the Methodist church believes it learns insight into the truth of God from those who say He was not crucified and was not the Son of God at all as the Qur'an says. This is the wrong approach. Yet this is the only statement of faith that could be found on their web site. From its web site it would seem this church has removed the centrality of Jesus death on the cross for our sins. If so it is ripe for serious further decline. It should be clarified that there is nothing wrong in engaging Muslims in debate as many Christians have done heroically with great results. What is wrong is any suggestion that Muslims and Christians are worshipping the same God and so learn about God from each other. It is not the purpose of this book to go into this further but there is plenty of evidence that Allah of the Qur'an is not the same as the God of the Bible.

The church says it is opposed to abortion and life starts at conception but when it asks the question "How does the Methodist church engage with politics?" Its' answer is "You can see the range of issues in which the Methodist Church has been active in recent years - including poverty and inequality, the environment and climate change, nuclear weapons and the harm caused by problem drinking." No mention of abortion or the family or transsexualism or assisted dying.

UK - United Reformed Church

Allows its ministers to conduct same sex marriages if they so wish. Their web site says current church attendance is just over 17,000 people in 1,406 churches, that is around 12 people per church.

The URC says in their statement of the Nature, Faith and Order of the United Reformed Church: -
"The highest authority for what we believe and do is God's Word in the Bible alive for his people today through the help of the Spirit. We respond to this Word, whose servants we are with all God's people." But then they allow ministers to conduct same sex marriages which is supporting sin and directly contrary to the word of God! So it is clear that the URC has departed from its heritage and is no longer following the teaching of Scripture.

Meanwhile Pentecostal churches have seen a big increase a rise of some 64% in 10 years to around 600,000. It is recorded that Pentecostal churchgoers now make up 32% of Sunday worshippers in London, compared to 27% for Catholics and 12% attending Anglican churches and the Anglican churches that are full are the Charismatic and Evangelical ones.

When the media talk about church attendance they only talk about the C of E. They never give the full picture.

Christianty.com says, "Because there are so many different sects of Pentecostals, beliefs tend to differ in some ways.

However, most of the churches share the same core beliefs that salvation is through Jesus, healing is possible through Him and He is returning again. Among the core tenants of Pentecostalism are: that most Pentecostals believe in medicine and doctors, but also strongly believe in divine healing. Most believe that baptism in the Holy Spirit begins when the person begins speaking in tongues. The belief stems from a literal interpretation of the Bible. One of those cited verses is Mark 16:17-18, which says that those who believe will be able to cast out demons, heal and speak in tongues. While it's hard to estimate just how many Pentecostals are in the world or even the United States, a Pew Research Centre study found that of the roughly two billion Christians in the world, about a quarter of that identifies as Pentecostal. After the Azusa revival, the handful of early Pentecostals swelled to more than 50,000 in just a few years. According to the New York Times, some four million Americans belong to classical Pentecostalism. Pentecostalism has long been considered one of the fastest and largest growing forms of Christianity." That's why when the media want to attack the church and say it is declining, they exclude Pentecostal congregations from their figures.

The Roman Catholic church.
From 2001 to 2010 the Holy See, the central governing body of the Catholic Church, considered sex abuse allegations

involving about 3,000 priests dating back fifty years. This year Pope Francis began by accusing victims of fabricating allegations, but by April was apologizing for his "tragic error" and by August was expressing "shame and sorrow" for the tragic history, without, however, introducing concrete measures either to prosecute abusers or to help victims. Generally, the church is strong on moral issues such as abortion and the family but weak on personal relationship with God. There is however a powerful charismatic group within the Catholic church where that certainly doesn't apply. Catholics generally believe that their church is the only true church which exalts denomination above belief.

There are other churches that don't fit easily into any of the headings given here. These are meant to be a broad cross section of what the church in the UK looks like right now. The state of most of these churches means that they are completely ill equipped to confront the Satanic Agenda but there is a sifting taking place. Jesus's messages to the churches in Revelation 2 and 3 is pertinent, "I know the blasphemy of those who say they are Jews and are not, but are a synagogue of Satan." (Rev 2:9) This could easily be read today "I know the blasphemy of those who say they are Christians and are not, but are a synagogue of Satan". The synagogue of Satan in church buildings is getting smaller and smaller while the true church of God is rising to take its place and when that happens the Satanic agenda will be in great peril.

The State of the Church in the UK

CHAPTER 5

Promoting the Christian Message in Politics

"The greatness of a man's power is the measure of his surrender."

William Booth

One of the amazing features of the Satanic agenda is the way the New Age organisation was set up about 150 years ago and then its programme was formulated about 80 years ago. Today we are seeing it being implemented. This is a lesson for us to think long term. Sadly, too often Godly churches are focussed on a Conference or crusade coming up and put enormous resources into it in a way that can never be repeated. That is not building anything. It is creating a bubble that bursts. We have to develop strategies and vision that can last down the generations that is directly from the heart of God.

The right approach is to track where we are now, recognise where God wants to take us, and plan a route to that end. We believe that God wants the Christian Peoples Alliance in Government, running this country, a process that is bound to take time. There is a temptation therefore to look at other established parties and to see them as a possible quick route to the same end.

This is the strategy that is offered by Christians in Politics. This is an umbrella group of Christians in the three main political parties. The ideal of these groups is that they would be standing boldly within their parties challenging the leadership to abandon the Satanic liberal agenda described above and instead follow God's will and plan and purposes and God's moral law. However, on whatever basis they were set up that is not what their parties want. They don't want pressure groups in their midst calling on them to change policy. They want groups that allow them to get votes from Christians for their party. The reality is that there aren't any groups in the main parties that are effective in making their party more Christian. In fact each party has become less and less Christian as their Christian Groups stand back and say nothing when anti-Christian legislation is proposed. It would appear that all the three groups below have abandoned being a pressure group and conformed to what their party wants. We shall now look at each in turn.

Conservative Christian Fellowship

The CCF has its offices at 4 Matthew Parker Street, London, SW1H 9HQ. That is the same office as the rest of the Conservative Party. When the CCF was set up it was an organisation outside of the party structure but sometime in the past they were called into the party headquarters and given offices close to that of the party chairman and leader. They were then told not to rock the boat but to support party policy. This led to the leader of CCF declaring at the height of the controversy over same sex marriage in 2013, "I don't want to talk about that". Another member who suggested that God wants us to leave the European Union was asked to keep quiet. That isn't official party policy so CCF can't say that even though a large number of Conservative MPs do. In recent years the party has changed dramatically from being a pro family party under Ian Duncan Smith to being a very socially liberal party now. It seems almost incredible that Ian Duncan Smith as Conservative leader had a 3-line whip compelling all Conservative MPs to vote against homosexual couples being allowed to adopt children. At the time one of the founders of CCF was in close support. Now Theresa May is declaring she will make the "abhorrent" practice of praying for homosexuals with unwanted same sex attraction illegal and the CCF is silent. This really is a nonsense position. Liberals welcome heterosexuals changing and becoming homosexuals. They call it "coming out". They say people can say they are unhappy in their gender and ask to change it. However, they say if you are homosexual you are born that way and cannot change under any circumstance. You are not born a boy or a girl or heterosexual and can change but you are born homosexual and cannot change according to this agenda! The CCF says nothing because they have abandoned being a Christian pressure group. There are a few Conservative MPs currently led by Fiona Bruce MP who do put God first, but they are a small minority and struggle to get their voice heard. They are very uncomfortable now in the modern Conservative Party. One reason the party found it so easy to shift course is its main reason for existence, which is to be in power. The party is quite happy to change policies if that is necessary to be in power and it was perceived rightly or wrongly that the media were so opposed to the Christian family agenda that if the Conservative Party continued to support it they would never get back into power. Principle takes a back seat to pragmatism and the CCF looks on and asks people to vote Conservative whatever their party's policies are on the grounds that perhaps another party is worse.

Christians on the Left

The roots of the Labour Party are in working class Christians. Kier Hardy their first MP fought to have the party called the party of labour rather than the socialist party. The party was formed out of a deep sense of grievance that the poorest in society didn't have a voice and they should have a voice. They gained power in the turmoil of the 1920s. Jesus always associated with the poor and marginalised and this is God's heart. Where did it all go wrong? It is hard to see exactly but certainly Tony Blair had a different approach from his predecessors. He decided to call the party "New Labour" mirroring the "New Age" philosophy talked about earlier. All that agenda was promoted by him plus a fanatical support for the EU. Christians on the Left used to be called the Christian Socialist Movement. There is no evidence at all that it in any way challenged Tony Blair. Apparently, they didn't even challenge him over the Iraq war which was obviously wrong from any Christian standpoint and the CPA certainly spoke out against at the time. We have had two Labour Councillors join us and both of them told us how in Labour circles they were banned from talking about same sex marriage or abortion or Islam or assisted dying. One Christian Labour MP described how he was terrified of his colleagues when assisted dying was being debated knowing he had to vote against it. Perhaps that is a clear indication how the soul of the party has become very anti-Christian. Christians on the Left say they are "a movement of Christians with a radical commitment to social justice, to protecting the environment and to fostering peace and reconciliation.... They have a sense that the global economic order needs re-wiring."

Absolutely Christians support social justice. Caring for the poor is one of the core values of the CPA, but it is also a core value of many other parties. We are also committed to protecting the environment as this is God's creation. Fostering peace and reconciliation is important though our focus would be more on justice and for peace to operate in the framework of justice. As for the global economic order Socialists take the approach that the economy is like a cake which if only it were divided up differently then we would have a fairer society. So, they tax the rich and business heavily. What they don't appreciate is that the economy isn't like a cake. It's like a train where the engine is business which creates money to employ people and to provide for the health service, education, welfare benefits etc. If you damage business by taxing it heavily you are damaging the engine which means everyone suffers. This is a severe weakness in the philosophy of Socialism repeated by Christians on the Left but their agenda has no reference at all to moral issues which are of supreme importance to Christians.

Lib Dem Christian Forum

Their web site tells us "We are Christians who support the Liberal Democrats. We believe that our faith can - and should - lead us to engage in the world of politics. We are passionate about many issues including social justice, the environment, freedom of conscience, international development, and the treatment of refugees. We join together to have a louder voice." Again, there is no mention of any of the moral issues like marriage, homosexuality, transsexualism or Islam. They are the party most recently to have a Christian as their leader in Tim Farron MP. However, Tim took the position that his job as leader was to support party policy whether he agreed with it or not. The media however wouldn't let him stop there. They hounded him to say, "do you personally believe homosexuality is sin?" He tried the best he could to avoid answering the question but finally gave in and said "No". Then he was forced to compromise on other issues as well. Finally, he was forced to resign by homosexuals in his party and in his resignation letter he said: - "From the very first day of my leadership, I have faced questions about my Christian faith. I've tried to answer with grace and patience. Sometimes my answers could have been wiser. At the start of this election, I found myself under scrutiny again - asked about matters to do with my faith. I felt guilty that this focus was distracting attention from our campaign, obscuring our message. Journalists have every right to ask what they see fit. The consequences of the focus on my faith is that I have found myself torn between living as a faithful Christian and serving as a political leader. A better, wiser person than me may have been able to deal with this more successfully, to have remained faithful to Christ while leading a political party in the current environment. To be a political leader - especially of a progressive, liberal party in 2017 - and to live as a committed Christian, to hold faithfully to the Bible's teaching, has felt impossible for me." So there we have it. Tim Farron said he cannot be faithful to Christ and lead the

Lib Dems. Where was the Lib Dem Christian Forum? Completely absent and silent as far as is known. If there is evidence they gave Tim Farron encouragement to stand firm for Christ we would love to be told how they spoke out condemning homosexuality and abortion when he was leader. So far there is nothing.

The fact that Christians in Politics have all agreed to be silent on moral issues that are really important to Christians means that the end result is that Christians all vote against one another and are completely ineffective in the political sphere. Rather than advancing the cause of Christianity in the main three parties Christians in Politics are managing retreat and putting up no fight at all at the battle front against the Satanic agenda. The crucial moral issues right now being debated in Parliament are transsexualism, the promotion of sex education to young children, the decriminalisation of abortion and attempts to ban Christians from standing outside abortion clinics to offer help to those going in. If Christians in Politics are silent on these issues they are of little value to the Christian community.

The only people that are currently allowed to be part of Christians in Politics are Conservative, Labour and Liberal members but we will look briefly at other parties.

The expulsion of Christina Summers, a Christian Green Councillor, for opposing same sex marriage in 2012 made it clear to the whole world that the Green party does not tolerate Christians. Green policies are socially and morally extreme.

It is not our job here to examine them in detail but suffice to say they want to close army bases in the UK and some military training areas and decommission them for use as nature reserves. They say we should rely totally on the United Nations for our defence. In 2015 their leader said it should be no crime to belong to Islamic State, al-Qaida or the IRA. They say however that homophobia, transphobia and biphobia should be "extinguished from society" and made hate crimes. So, it should not be a crime to be a member of an organisation that beheads Christians and engages in wanton violence, but it should be a crime to criticise homosexuality in Green thinking.

We don't know of any Christian Group in the party. There is an organisation called Green Christian that campaigns on environmental issues, but it does not appear to be linked to the Green Party.

UKIP went down the liberal route and accepted the liberal agenda under Nigel Farage but then appeared to reign back from that position after the party fractured following Nigel Farage's departure. Now since Gerald Batten took over its leadership it has not expressed any support for liberalism. However, the party never speaks on moral issues other than

Islam. On Islam it speaks from a very abrasive perspective showing no understanding of our call to love Muslims while condemning what Muhammad stood for. The party has also been willing to make racist statements like "Romanians and Bulgarians are responsible for all the increase in crime in this country" which is labelling two nations as criminals very unfairly. Having said that Christian Soldiers UKIP does seem to adopt a very strong Christian position. It would appear it is a Christian voice in the party unafraid to speak out and seeking to get UKIP to adopt Christian policies unlike the Christian groups in all the other parties.

The SNP in Scotland and Plaid Cymru in Wales are adopting extreme liberal positions and Christians appear to have little influence in those parties. The DUP from Northern Ireland is the only party in the current House of Commons that stands against same sex marriage and abortion and against the EU and adopts a strongly Christian position on just about every issue. DUP members are also very committed to prayer and it is a pleasure to work with them when we can.

Overall being a Christian in any party other than the CPA or DUP involves some measure of compromise. In some parties like Labour, Lib Dem, Greens or the Nationalists it would seem almost impossible to stand 100% for God. The Conservatives and UKIP show a greater toleration of Christian values but still tend to marginalise Christians often using deception in the process. Uniquely in Great Britain the CPA is committed as a party to putting the will of God first in its thinking. There is not a single group in any other party outside Northern Ireland that puts God's will first in their thinking though there are individual MPs that do. Most put their party's interest first. That way Christianity can never advance and on the contrary will always be in retreat.

One of the arguments of Christians in Politics is that the CPA will never be in power. They just might be wrong but in any case, in the interim we can gain influence massively. The reader should reflect that before the Green Party (or Ecology Party) existed environment issues were hardly discussed. When they started to get a lot of votes suddenly all the other parties wanted to show their Green credentials. It was because UKIP started to get a lot of votes and threatened a serious breakthrough that David Cameron promised a referendum on the EU to head off their support. If UKIP had never existed, we would never have had an EU referendum in 2016. The reality is that if the CPA starts to get a lot of votes the first thing is that the other parties will start to react to head off the support we are getting and to try and show their Christian credentials. At the moment they are more interested in winning Muslim votes than Christian votes as Muslims are seen to have more influence than Christians over the number of votes parties get. A vote for the CPA will be a vote for greater Christian influence even if the CPA candidate doesn't win.

Church Support for CPA

In the next chapter we will look in detail at the CPA manifesto and lay it open on the table for anyone to say any proposal is not according to the will of God as far as they are concerned. We aim always to glorify God in all we say and do. Some Christian groups and churches have caught the vision. However, support for the CPA among churches and Christian groups is varied. The list below is not exhaustive but reflects organisations we have had dealings with. If your group is not mentioned here or is not yet opening its doors to us, then we would always welcome an open door to talk and share the CPA vision.

Group 1. Total Support for the CPA and a belief that God wants to raise up the CPA to run the nation and are actively praying to that end

IPAA (Inter Prophetic and Apostolic Alliance)
Voice of Prophecy
Solemn Assembly
Spontaneous Worship
City Chapel
House of Ishmael Ministries

Peculiar People Ministries

Group 2. Freely offers CPA a platform and are happy to advertise what it stands for

Christian Concern
Day of Prayer for Britain
Global Christian Fellowship
SPUC
Abort 67
Revelation TV
Faith TV
Olive TV
Prayer for Parliament

Group 3. Those that have indicated some support for CPA but not yet offered any significant platform

Global Day of Prayer (There have been many opportunities, but CPA has never been given a platform)
Trumpet Call (A video with me speaking was used to promote Trumpet Call 2018)
March for Life (We were told we applied too late for 2018. We hope to be on the platform in future)
Ruach. (We have had a stand and a Ruach member stood for us and was interviewed at a Ruach women's conference.)

KICC (Support has been offered in past years but not recently)

RCCG (Support was offered by leaders in Nigeria but there has been no open door in the UK)

UCB (Sympathy has been shown with what we stand for but no interview has been given)

City Gates (The leadership has encouraged members to campaign for us in the past)

Group 4. Closed doors to CPA at the moment

Evangelical Alliance
New Wine
Movement UK
Premier Radio

These last groups mostly promote Christians in Politics. We should clarify in our view it should be perfectly possible to promote both CPA and Christians in Politics at least as far as we are concerned. At the time of writing this book we have never been on a platform with Christians in Politics or debated with them or related to their current leaders. It maybe they work against us behind the scenes. As far as we are concerned, they are promoting their parties and we promote ours and we have very different roles to play and no Christian group has any reason to exclude the CPA from their meetings. We did buy a stand at a New Wine event but found significant hostility to what we stood for at fringe meetings and from the organisation. We were a very long way from getting on the platform and there was a closed door to us being invited to speak at any fringe meetings even though New Wine appeared to want to engage with political and moral issues. We were refused a stand at Movement UK as were Abort 67 both of us only operating outside the meetings. Christians in Politics had book tables and were very involved in fringe meetings. We gate crashed one Premier Radio recording by sitting in the audience and talking about the CPA from there but we have never been invited onto any programme. It seems that they are happy to debate tough questions on some of their programmes but don't want the CPA involved to express a view. This seems rather strange as the Christian body that is most committed to thinking and praying about political issues. Revelation TV has certainly welcomed our input enormously and we are very grateful to them. Other TV channels mentioned have given us occasional programmes.

Overall it is heartening that organisations most committed to prayer and seeking the will of God are most supportive of the CPA. The groups that aren't open to the CPA, to the extent that they are interested in politics, are more focused on discussion and debate though they have chosen not to involve us in that debate. Still closed doors today may be open doors tomorrow and we pray God will continue to open many new doors. We love to pray but are very willing to debate as well.

There are several organisations we have had dealings with that are not mentioned here mostly because we have only had one or two points of contact and at this stage don't know how the relationship will develop. That doesn't mean we aren't grateful for all opportunities we have had to appear on platforms and to meet church leaders one to one. We hope that as time goes by many more groups will appear in Group 1 and some will transfer from their current position to groups 1 or 2.

Finally, we are now working closely with the Christian Party and at the time of writing seeking a full merger. We are also seeking to get closer to the DUP and praying God will open that door further.

Promoting the Christian Message in Politics

CHAPTER 6

Developing a Christian Manifesto

While women weep, as they do now, I'll fight; while little children go hungry, as they do now, I'll fight; while men go to prison, in and out, in and out, as they do now, I'll fight; while there is a drunkard left, while there is a poor lost girl upon the streets, while there remains one dark soul without the light of God, I'll fight-I'll fight to the very end!"
- William Booth

This is of necessity a long drawn out affair. It may be tempting just to focus on the moral issues and say that these are all we are concerned about. However, such does not give a platform for a political party to win an election. What we need to do is to face every political issue as it arises and seek God's heart for that. We are not claiming this manifesto is perfect, but we are claiming that in developing it we have sought the heart of God and there is much in here which is revelation from God. Our manifestos are constantly being updated and our latest manifesto is to be found on our web site, www.cpaparty.net. This chapter however gives the platform on which thirty-one Christian Peoples Alliance candidates stood in 2017. As such it remains permanently a document over 5,000 people voted for. It covers the following areas: -

Leader's Introduction
Basic Principles
Brexit
Wealth Creation and Employment
Free Efficient Health Service
Taxation Must be Fair
Defence and Foreign Policy
Greening the Economy and Transport
Reform the Banking System
Immigration
Refugees and Asylum Seekers

Unaccompanied Children
Economic/Educational Immigrants
People Trafficking
Illegal Immigrants
Other Moral Issues
The importance of marriage
The Sanctity of Life
Adoptive families
Further Family Support
Youth Policy
The sanctity of life from conception to natural death
Care for the Less Able
Issues relating to those on Low Incomes, including the Elderly
Morally Framed Education
Integration Agenda
Crime, Punishment and Restorative Justice
Housing and Development
The Political Process

Leader's Introduction

In Brexit, we face the biggest challenge in the UK's history since the reconstruction of the country after 1945.

Whilst we support much of Theresa May's approach thus far, it is abundantly clear that the EU will never negotiate good terms for our withdrawal. They do not want other countries to leave on the same terms. So they will seek to give us the worst terms possible. Indeed, we are already seeing this with an attempt to land us with a bill for £39 billion before they will start 'trade talks'.

'No deal' maybe a 'worst case' scenario – but, in order to succeed in any negotiation, it is necessary to look at, and prepare for, the 'worst case' scenario. And, that 'worse case' has a significant downside for the EU. For, with a committed budget of £135 billion (2017), the other 8 net contributing countries will have to find immediately that £7 billion to replace the net contribution from the UK.

But while (thus far) we largely support Theresa May's approach to the EU, this election is not only about the EU. Consequently, unlike this Tory Government, we would:

Divert the £50 billion being spent on maintaining and renewing Trident into a missile defence system.

Introduce a 5% Turnover Tax to ensure large multi-nationals pay their way in our society.

Ensure that benefits for the disabled and mentally ill are maintained not removed.

Provide emergency benefits for applicants while their claim is being assessed.

Reallocate foreign aid to those who really need it – e.g. refugees in camps – and away from nuclear powers or those countries which persecute Christians e.g. the £486 million to Pakistan.

Support marriages and families whose breakdown is costing the nation £48 billion a year.

Have a pro-life stance, saving 186,000 babies a year.

Those are just some of the reasons why the Christian Peoples Alliance is standing candidates in this election - to put forward positive ways of helping the most vulnerable in our nation, not just speak about it or pay 'lip-service' to those we meet in the streets.

But effectively supporting the most vulnerable requires a complete change from Labour's policies. And so, unlike Jeremy Corbyn, the CPA is committed to: -

- a sound economy in which top earners prosper and pay their tax – rather than having excessive tax rates;
- an effective NHS delivering excellent patient care and outcomes, regardless of whether that is by state, voluntary or private providers; and
- an effective education service with improving standards for <u>all</u> pupils, state and public.

The country is crying out for coherent opposition to the Conservative inability to understand how the poorest in society are affected by their policies. That is where we come in. We have clear coherent alternative that will help the poor and the elderly, improve services, and at the same time support and encourage business.

So, in this Manifesto, the Christian Peoples Alliance set out a fresh vision for an alternative society and I commend it to you.

Sid Cordle MBE
Leader, Christian Peoples Alliance

Basic Principles

The Christian Peoples Alliance sets out in this manifesto a fresh vision for an alternative society. A society based upon 6 principles, each and all of which work in harmony together to produce a happier, healthier and economically more prosperous society. These principles are:

The Effective Use of Resources
The Empowerment of the Individual and Communities
Active Compassion
Reconciliation
Respect for Life
Social Justice

This is not the capitalism of Conservatism or the Socialism of Labour; it is not the licence of the Liberal Democrats or the isolationism of UKIP, and it does not fit under any 'right', 'left' or 'centre' label. Instead it is a distinct political philosophy, proposing actual solutions to current issues in order to increase the vitality and well-being of <u>all</u> in our society.

In the following pages we will set out how these principles, as utilised by the CPA, will positively affect all aspects of life in Britain.

Before doing so we set out our five key policies for the 2017 Election:

1) Brexit -   to engage in good faith in substantive negotiations with the rest of the EU while being prepared to walk away if necessary. Use the opportunity of Brexit to transform our key industries.

2) 5% Turnover Tax -   to be levied on all sales in the UK above a fixed turnover level, so that tax is collected from those multi-nationals who divert their UK earnings to low-tax regimes by 'licence fees' or 'invoice address'.

3) Cancellation of Trident - with the up to £50 billion saving being used to invest in a missile shield and other key public services.

4) Dealing with Air Pollution -   to save the approx. 40,000 early deaths every year in the UK, and improving the quality of life of many.

5) Supporting Traditional Marriage - Supporting couples when they get married both financially and with training and also again when they have their first child.

We now turn to these, and our other policies, in greater detail.

Brexit

The greatest challenges we face over the lifetime of the next Parliament are the Brexit Negotiations and the after effects once we have left the EU.

Before commencing negotiations, we need to recognise that the Referendum Result, followed by the serving of the Article 50 Notice, have had a serious effect on those who remain in the EU. For we have rejected them and the federalist concept of power gravitating to the centre. Instead we have opted for the concept of a separate sovereign state that will live in cooperation with, but not ruled by, other external states. But this has caused hurt and, in places, anger from some. As we are already seeing from their initial 'negotiating stance' they will seek to impose hard or even impossible terms for our withdrawal, both because they are hurt but also to discourage other countries from leaving the EU.

Consequently, it is imperative that relationships between Britain and the other 27 states be improved. This does not mean going back on Brexit – the country made its decision on 23 June 2016 – but by taking moral and practical steps to take some of the angst out of the situation, the CPA would:

*Grant full rights of residence and work to all EU citizens who can show they are resident in the UK as at the date of publication of this Manifesto, Thursday 18 May 2017.

*Grant full rights of residence to all EU citizens who are married to or in a civil partnership with (or have booked weddings or civil partnerships) as at the date of publication of this Manifesto.

*Enter into Brexit Negotiations in good faith on the basis that these are not a 'zero-sum game' i.e. that a successful negotiation will end with both the UK and the EU ending up in a better place than if the negotiations break down. Those negotiations will not, however, be on the 27 States' basis that a financial settlement must be reached before trade talks can be started but that all matters must be discussed at the same time in parallel talks. If that is not acceptable to the 27 States, or if no acceptable deal can be reached on the basis set out below, then the CPA would repeal the European Communities Act 1972 and exit the EU without paying a penny more into its coffers from the date of our exit, falling back on World Trade Organisation rules. That would leave the 27 States with an approx. £7billion a year hole to plug from Day One.

The matters to be agreed include: -

A mutually beneficial trade agreement between the UK and countries within the EU. The EU exports £89 billion of goods per year more to the UK than the UK does to the EU ; whilst the UK exports £28 billion per year more in services to the EU.

An effective 'soft border; between Northern Ireland and the Republic of Ireland and an equivalent 'soft' border between Gibraltar and Spain though the effectiveness of these will have to be monitored.

UK parliamentary control of UK borders

The UK Supreme Court being the supreme court for the UK UK control of the seas around the UK for up to 200 miles or half way to the nearest country as per internationally agreed rules.

The CPA would also plan for a post-Brexit future by: -

*Investigating the possibility of trade agreements with other countries. In particular, with the new economic powerhouses of China, India, Brazil and Russia. These may be direct one-to-one or in partnership e.g. New Zealand lamb production and UK lamb production are at different times of the year, leading to the possibility of a combined export throughout the year to a third country. It is this type of new, co-operative, thinking that is needed.

*Invest in major industries (steel, ship building, car, energy etc) to increase efficiency and increase production in a sustainable manner. As John Longworth, Director General or British Chamber of Commerce said in August 2014 "We need to invest and export more, innovate and build".

*Continue agricultural subsidies for the first 5 years after Brexit so as to provide continuity for farmers, whilst discussing with farmers the phasing out of subsidies and the availability of capital injection to improve efficiency.

*Maintain other EU grants for a minimum of 3 years (unless they were due to finish earlier).

*Invest in research and development and then patenting and implementation of new products (e.g. graphene).

*Invest in UK infrastructure, in particular High-Speed Rail and a new London airport in the Thames Estuary with related links

*Conduct a review of all PFI contracts (hospitals, schools, government buildings etc) to ensure that they are providing value for money, introducing primary legislation if needed to rectify those contracts where excessive charges or profits are being made at the expense of society. (Since we wrote that the Government has done the review and stopped any new contracts a move we very much support)

Whenever the Government puts money into an industry it will do it alongside the private sector by giving capital grants and taking a share in the industry in proportion to the investment made. It is not our aim for the State to take over our industries but to support and help them grow and give them a boost. We anticipate that by taking this approach the Government will be increasing wealth for itself as well as for the country as a whole.

These policies are practical outworking of the basic Christian Democratic principles of effective use of resources, the empowerment of the individual and communities and will lead to an increase in social justice as the (currently) more disadvantaged areas of the UK will be improved.

At this point it is worth recording what we also said in our 2014 European manifesto: -

Under the heading "The CPA Position on the EU as it is Now" we said then: -

The CPA is calling for a referendum on remaining in the EU and if the vote was taken tomorrow would be campaigning to leave the EU. Until then and so long as we are part of the EU we will be working with other Christians in the European Christian Political Movement to bring about moral and democratic reform.

The idea that Britain has to remain in the EU and has to accept all its myriad of regulations is palpably false. Statistics show clearly that by 1990 our growth in the EU had declined to zero. The mass of new regulations have hurt our economy and the growth in our exports has been more outside than inside the EU. It was only after we left the ERM (Exchange Rate Mechanism) in 1992 that growth increased.

It is now absolutely clear that we are better off outside the single currency, though the Labour and Liberal Democrat Parties and many in the Conservative Party wanted us to join the euro. One of the main arguments for this was that if the European Central Bank were situated in Frankfurt, and Britain was not a member of European Monetary Union, the financial centre of London would lose its importance. In fact in the latest Global Financial Centres Index (GFCI 12)

London is not only still rated first, it has improved its lead over New York. Frankfurt is rated thirteenth its rating having declined and it is also behind 2 European cities that have never been in the EU, Zurich and Geneva. Frankfurt is not among the 10 centres likely to become more significant. London is, despite already being top. Neither is Frankfurt among the top 10 centres where financial institutions say new offices will be opened. London is third. The cities that have really lost out are Paris (29th) and Amsterdam (31st) which are in the eurozone.

Economically Britain has gained enormously by having an inflation target instead of an exchange rate target since 1992. This is what has led to a stable currency and stable low interest rates. The CPA will examine the facts and speak out the truth. There is no economic argument left for us to join the euro. There are massive economic arguments for us to keep the pound.

The idea that only a federal structure can keep the peace in Europe has been shown to be palpably false by the way the Federal Republic of Yugoslavia disintegrated amid massive bloodshed. The breakup of the old Soviet Union is another example. A federal structure therefore is no more likely to solve conflicts than any other. Rather, history has shown democracy to be the most effective means of ensuring peace between nations. Rarely has there been war between two democracies. The EU, however, is undermining the democratic relationship between the nation states and the people they represent by imposing laws with no democratic mandate.

We then said, "The key reasons we were told we had to be in the EU in the first place, economic gain and keeping the peace in Europe have therefore both been shown to be false. Furthermore, we must also leave the EU for the following reasons: -

1 Corruption. In the last audit 4.8% of the EU budget was missing. That amounts to £5.4billion, more than the whole budget of the United Nations. This is an increase from 3.9% last year so the problem far from being dealt with is getting worse. For 19 years now, vast amounts of money have been missing from the EU budget. If this were a company it would be put into forcible liquidation as a result. This money is coming into the EU; someone must know where it is going. When 640 million euros was found missing from Eurostat (the EU statistics agency), in 2003 the action taken was completely inadequate.

2 Failure to respect the Christian heritage of Europe. The whole focus of Europe has been on human rights legislation. Some of this is good but it has also been used to shift us away from Christian values of right and wrong, good and evil. These values are the true foundation of authentic human rights. They have underpinned our laws down the centuries and are being eroded. When the draft constitution was produced in 2004 several countries led by Italy, Poland and Spain wanted it to respect Europe's Christian heritage, but they were voted down.

3 Lack of Democracy. Only the Commission can initiate legislation in Europe. The Council of Ministers and the European Parliament can only agree or disagree with what the Commission proposes. The Commission also controls the executive in Europe, its civil servants. It is totally unelected. Is has been said of the current British Commissioner, Baroness Ashton, that she has never been elected to anything. More often it is made up of politicians who have lost elections or resigned from office like her predecessors Leon Brittain, Neil Kinnock and Peter Mandelson. "Unaccountable politicians" as they have been called."

Finally, we said, "We are therefore now faced with a likelihood that sometime soon there will be a referendum on our continued membership of the EU and a likelihood that when it is held the majority in the UK will vote "No". The next question is therefore what sort of country will we be outside the EU and which is the best party to take us into that future? It is our contention that the old parties of the Conservatives, Labour and the Liberal Democrats, who have all deceived the British people over a long period, cannot now be the champions of a new Britain outside the EU.

Equally UKIP's vision for us of a nation that cancels all Overseas Aid, blames foreigners for crime and supports nationalism, does not provide the prospect of a Government the majority of British Citizens would want to live under. The CPA offers a different vision and one that can unite the nation within the freedom of open debate and discussion."

We then spend several pages saying what changes we want to make when the UK leaves the EU. What we say can be read now on our web site under policies, https://cpaparty.net/wp-content/uploads/2018/10/CPA-Euro-Manifesto-2014-150908.pdf. No other party actually expected us to vote to leave the EU and no other party had done any work on the process of leaving or what changes they want to make.

We now return to the 2017 CPA manifesto.

Wealth Creation and Employment

These policies will also result in increased wealth, whether due to the effects of capital investment spreading down through the economy or the increased innovation and efficiency of UK production or the new trade routes opened up. That wealth must be spread throughout society. To this end the CPA will: -

*Change the responsibility of company directors, such that they must consider best balanced interests to shareholders, employees, suppliers, the local community and wider society, with that being considered in a business process audit to be carried out and published every three years. This process audit to include rating of executives.

*Bonuses to be paid to everyone in a company, proportionate to their basic salary so the benefit flows out to wider society. If bonuses are paid only to executives, then they will be taxed at 80% to give a strong incentive for this practice to cease.

*Company share schemes must be allocated on the same basis to all employees (who have been employed for more than 2 years) with employee shares having enhanced voting rights, giving a greater say to employees in how their company is run. Again we will give a strong tax incentive to encourage this behaviour.

*Reforming taxation on capital allowances so as to simplify the system and concentrate it on future expenditure by barring claims for pre-April 2012 expenditure.

These policies are designed to encourage both the effective use of resources and social justice, whilst empowering the individual.

Free Efficient Health Service

The CPA is committed to: -
*A publicly funded, effective and value for money National Health Service.
*One that promotes health and well-being and provides the best possible outcomes.
*One that is free at the point of delivery for all UK citizens.
*One that is patient focussed, with integrated health care on a geographical basis.
*Finally one that has adequate additional funding for improvements to health and social care.

The CPA is completely committed to providing emergency treatment to all who need it, without first requiring payment. Whilst health insurance will be required by all coming to the UK the CPA will require payment or proof of insurance after emergency treatment or before non-emergency treatment, but subject always to that not affecting the wellbeing of the patient.
The CPA is committed to increase the health and well-being of all residing in the UK by providing high quality health care when needed, regardless of through whom that is

provided – the State, a charity or voluntary organisation or a private company. The CPA will seek to encourage and facilitate differing forms of partnership suitable for local circumstances by the NHS with local authorities, charities, non-profit and for-profit organisations and, above all, with patients.

These partnerships will include: -
*Prevention and self-cure programmes – in particular relating to smoking, obesity and exercise, workplace health schemes and incentives, alcohol, excess sugar and salt.

*Planning treatment (including prevention) in conjunction with individuals (who are often experts by experience) so that it is an agreed course of action to which they are fully subscribed.

*Involving carers fully in that planning including respite planning providing integrated health care on an appropriate geographical basis, breaking down the current barriers between primary and secondary care.

*Promoting holistic patient centred care.

*A more effective dovetailing of urgent and emergency care from NHS 111 and GP out of hours service through the 999 and ambulance service urgent care centres to full A&E and major trauma centres, such that the patient gets the most appropriate treatment at the appropriate level, quickest.

*Encouraging and facilitating out-of-hospital services (including GPs and community services) to find appropriate ways within their communities of working at scale, whilst still maintaining the personal link with 'my GP'.

*Running further pilot schemes with locally integrated health and social care funding and clinical support, so that care homes and intermediate care homes can provide more appropriate beds at a lower cost whilst still having the support there if required, whilst freeing up several thousand beds for actual acute use.

*Integration of physical and mental health aspects of care, with parity of esteem and 24-hour mental health teams in all A&E departments by 2020.

*Enable additional work to take place between the NHS and the voluntary sector to increase the provision of good quality terminal and palliative and respite care for infants, children and adults, whether in their own homes or in hospices. This care will be benchmarked against the world's best examples of each.

The CPA will consult with the NHS about the most effective way of reducing bureaucracy, increasing efficiency and managing change so that the core principles of empowering individuals and local communities and the effective use of resources are dovetailed in with respect for life, social justice and active compassion.

In this vein other matters that the CPA considers to be important for the NHS are: -

a) Encourage nurse training to contain an increased sense of vocation and practical training.

b) Have national standards of healthcare rather than targets.

c) Restore a pro-life ethic across the NHS so that every member of staff is doing their best to assist the healing of a patient and where life is coming to an end, to provide the best care and quality of life.

d) Improve the means for staff to identify and report their concerns about quality of care and patient safety without fear of recrimination for whistle blowing.

e) Institute a no-fault liability system to allow members of staff to admit to mistakes. This will do three things: -

* Allow any system malfunction and rectification to the benefit of future patients. Such a 'system malfunction' may be a member of staff who needs retraining or additional training, or being moved to other duties.

*Allow for the speedy compensation of the impaired patient, without a lengthy legal battle in which the medical professional/institution seek to deny liability.

*Remove the expensive legal costs in fighting such cases which can be far more than the compensation. This in itself will be a saving of £418 million (2015-16) for claimants' lawyers as well as the money spent by the NHS on its lawyers.

f) Enhance the voice of the patient and improve responsiveness to patients and public by improving the NHS complaints process.

g) Enhance the capability and capacity of the NHS to plan and deliver appropriate change without calling on expensive external consultants, including increasing the influence of healthcare professional bodies, health staff and patient groups; and so restore responsibility for health planning to public health and clinical leaders.

h) Use the purchasing power of the NHS to get the best deals for all NHS procurement.

i) Encourage the Royal College of Paediatrics and Child Health to put the symptoms of Type 1 diabetes in the red book given to new parents. A child is five times more likely to be diagnosed with type 1 diabetes than meningitis, yet the symptoms are not documented in the red baby book that every new parent is given.

We will also ensure respect for older people and the people with long-term illnesses by working towards state funded personal care for the elderly and disabled people. As part of our 'partnership' proposals domiciliary home care services must be improved and the option of sheltered accommodation should be made available where it is the right solution for an elderly person. Where the best solution is for an elderly person to move in with a relative or close friend, we would assess the possibility of a grant towards the cost of adapting the new premises or putting in an appropriate support package. The CPA would also reward those who stay at home to look after an elderly parent by increasing the Carers Allowance substantially from £62.70 per week and not linking it to any other benefit. We would consult on how that may be increased due to age or frailty increasing as time passes.

Public Support

It will be essential that this programme of enhanced health care receives public support so changes are not seen simply as a 'cost-cutting exercise'.

In order to do this the CPA will: -

*Propose an <u>increase</u> to the NHS budget contingent upon, and commensurate with, these improvements in health care taking place.

*Encourage engagement and genuine consultation with local populations as well as health professionals.

*Require improvements in local health care to be experienced before there is a transfer of resources; and encourage personal participation – in personal prevention programmes, membership of health boards or volunteering within the community.

In keeping with the core principles of the CPA, these improvements need to be, and be seen as, empowering individuals and local communities whilst being a more effective use of resources for a more effective health service with better outcomes.

Finance

The CPA would provide adequate funding for the NHS as it currently is. It will, however, require additional funding. There are two aspects of this. First an element of 'double funding' whilst the new schemes are being put in place and, second, to cover the annual funding gap from that which the NHS currently provides to an NHS fit for the UK for the 21st Century. This last is estimated at £30 billion a year by 2020/21. We will however reduce the burden on the NHS by encouraging family stability the breakdown of which is anticipated to cost the nation £48bn per year a significant part of which is cost to the NHS.

The NHS should also be able to make demand and efficiency savings (cutting back on duplication of services, providing better outcomes more efficiently by utilising staff and resources in new ways) of 2% - 3% per annum (currently 1.6% per annum). This would allow the current anticipated future annual £30 billion funding gap (2020/21)to be bridged.

Utilising the sugar and salt tax for health purposes. The existing sugar tax is expected to raise £1 billion which goes to the Department of Education for school sports (ie well-being and prevention of obesity). The new taxes would not apply immediately (see Taxation below), but reliably may be expected to raise more than £1 billion a year. This would assist if the NHS efficiencies do not produce 2% - 3% per annum as currently envisaged.

Taxation Must be Fair

Concretely the Christian Peoples Alliance is committed to seeking to balance the Government's books over the medium term. To this end it will be necessary to review the regulatory system and quangos. All the current measures will need to remain in force when we leave the EU but we do not have to keep any of them unless required to by a trade agreement. We will need to keep what is working and repeal what is not useful. The Christian Peoples Alliance wants a much reduced regulatory system in every industry which we believe can lead to lower taxation, but this review has to be conducted in an orderly and thorough fashion and there has to be an appeals system both for and against regulations that is thorough and robust.

In the meantime, there is an anomaly in the tax system which must be corrected. In 2016/17 the taxation is as follows:-

Tax 0% £10,600 Nat Ins 0% £8,060

Tax 20%   £42,600   Nat Ins Employee 12% to £43,004 Employer 14%

Tax 40% £42,600 to £160,600 Nat. Ins Employee 2% Employer 14%
Tax45% over £160,600 Nat. Ins 2% Employer 14%.
(Normally when the Government gives the rates it gives them as the rate above the tax threshold so gives a 20% rate of up to £32,000 of additional income and 45% rate over £150,000. We have given the rate on total earnings)

For self-employed people there is a standing class 2 National Insurance payment to make of £2.80 a week and 9% on profits up to £43,000 2% above that. Tax is the same.

From this it can be seen that as soon as the tax rate climbs from 20% to 40% the National Insurance reduces so the marginal increase is 10% not 20%.

We propose as follows:-
Tax 0% £10,600 Nat Ins 0% £10,600
Tax 20% £42,600 Nat Ins Employee 12% , Employer 14%
Tax 30% £42,600 to £100,600 Nat. Ins Employee 12% Employer 14%
Tax 40% over £100,600 Nat. Ins 12% Employer 14%.

For self-employed people we propose a standing class 2 payment to make of £2.80 and 9% on all profits above £10,600.

The effect of this will be that everyone earning less than £100,000 will be £507 per year better off. For those earning £5,000 to £10,000 per year this will be a higher percentage of their income. People earning between £100,000 and £160,000 will be up to £5,500 per year worse off and people earning over £160,000 will be £5,500 worse off plus 5% of their remaining salary. For self-employed people the new 30% band will mean those earning between £41,865 and £100,000 will be up to £1,744.05 per year better off, but those earning above £100,000 will progressively lose this benefit and start to pay more at a rate of 7% of their earnings.

This measure will take a big step towards combining tax and national insurance and so making tax simpler. It will also make the real tax rate paid much more transparent. It will give the greatest help to the lowest paid. If at the same time we are able to reduce tax rates we will.

The CPA will introduce a Turnover Tax' initially set at 5% of turnover, payable quarterly in arrears along with VAT. We will consult on the minimum level of turnover to which this will apply but it is intended to ensure that appropriate tax is collected from those multi-national companies who make their money by selling in the UK but transfer their profits overseas by way of 'licence' and other 'costs' or 'invoice address'.

Turnover Tax

The total turnover of the UK economy in 2016 was £1.976 trillion. 5% of that is £98bn. It would be offset against Corporation tax which raised £56bn in 2016/17 and small companies would be exempt and we would probably introduce other exemptions which would take away about £20bn. Some corporation tax would be more than the turnover tax, but we estimate that will would leave us net at least £30bn.

Other Taxation Measures

The CPA will also work with other countries to require 'country by country' reporting by companies; open records of beneficial ownership to be available, and to increase the automatic exchange of financial accounting information between different tax jurisdictions. The CPA will start with the Crown Dependencies and British Overseas Territories, where these do not already conform to these requirements. The CPA considers that the current framework, by which individuals and companies can avoid paying their fair share of tax, causes the costs of running our society to fall disproportionally onto the shoulders of others. This must be brought to an end.

We will also review the effectiveness of the Government's reduction in Corporation Tax. If it has indeed been effective in getting businesses to relocate to the UK we will do nothing to stop that process. If not then large businesses should not avoid paying their fair share. We will introduce a reduced rate of half the normal rate for companies involved in manufacturing as the Irish have done to great positive effect. We need to encourage the growth of manufacturing in the UK and this measure will do a lot to encourage large manufacturing companies to base themselves here.

Stamp duty land tax changed from 1st April 2016 very much along the lines we proposed in our 2015 manifesto. It wasn't in the Conservative Party manifesto. It is welcome that they implemented our manifesto on this issue rather than theirs. We would now change it further to introduce another SDLT rate above £4,000,000 at 20%.

Where commercial or residential properties are being produced as income producing investments (eg buy-to-let) the SDLT would be 20%. The effect of this would be to decrease the price paid by the investor, leading to cheaper flats and houses for occupation and in the commercial field rebalancing of the price received by the seller and that received by the community.

Although we are not in favour of a 'mansion tax' that would adversely affect those who are income poor but live in a large house (often for historic or sentimental reasons), a revaluation of the Council Tax Bands is now well overdue. We would schedule this for mid-way through the next Parliament, with new bands being introduced at £500,000 and every £250,000 thereafter to £5,000,000. This will allow for the re-adjustment of relative prices in different areas across the UK since the 1 April 1991 valuation some 26 years ago. We would consult on the mitigation of any consequential effects on the 'income poor' following such a revaluation.

We will review the inheritance tax levels to see if they are working effectively. Rather than a flat 40% rate we favour a scaled increase starting at 20% and then rising to 30% and 40% for larger inheritances. We would seek to maintain the overall revenue from inheritance tax and possibly increase it if we can.

The Government has also introduced the tax we proposed in our 2015 manifesto on drinks which contain sugar. We welcome that but would now go further and put a tax on all foods that contain salt and processed sugar (other than home produced cakes, jam etc sold for charity or non-profit causes). These taxes will take effect after a period, to be decided after consultation, allowing the food industry to decrease salt and sugar levels gradually over that time, whilst allowing individuals' tastes to become accustomed to the change.

We will clamp down on tax avoidance by making it illegal to offset losses from one company against the profit of another. In future each company will have to be stand alone and if necessary loss making companies will have to close down. At the moment some people have created loss making companies as a way of tax avoidance.

Company pension schemes will continue to be given tax relief and encouraged but a threshold will be placed on the amount of tax free benefit that can be paid into a Company pension scheme for an employee at £30,000 per tax year without incurring corporation tax. Sometimes these benefits have been used to make enormous payments to executives tax free. If those executives are over 55 they can effectively be receiving a massive tax free payment as 25% of the fund could immediately be drawn tax free. The idea of promoting Company pensions is to help those in retirement across the board not as a tax loophole.

We continue to be appalled by the scandal of tax evasion and fraud that robs our society of the money it needs. It is now clear that the HSBC tax scandal involved 30,000 people and the Government were first informed of it in 2009. Then there is the Missing Trader Intra Community (MTIC) Tax fraud which has been going on unchecked for over 15 years and involves HMRC giving over £1 billion in VAT refunds to fraudsters. We will institute a full public inquiry into these scandals with prosecutions to the guilty. The cost of the enquiry will be nothing compared with the money that can be regained. Labour's call to ask HMRC to clamp down on tax fraud has not worked and will not work so an outside investigation is needed.

These policies are also designed to further social justice, whilst empowering the individual and encouraging the effective use of resources.

Defence and Foreign Policy

"The Christian Peoples Alliance seeks international peace and security by multilateral security initiatives reducing the amount of armaments in the world and reducing the international arms trade starting with our own.

The danger of a nuclear weapons exchange by intention or accident remains a credible possibility and nuclear proliferation among nations and into terrorist groups must be prevented. Nuclear weapon states must take practical steps to nuclear disarmament and thereby prevent nuclear weapon proliferation in accordance with the Non-Proliferation Treaty. The CPA believes that it would never be a Christian act to use weapons of mass destruction, nor ask others to do it on their behalf. We would cancel the Trident renewal programme, utilising the savings to refocus defence spending.

We believe that the focus of our defence spending should be on developing defensive systems including missile shields round the UK. We must work with other countries in Europe to achieve an effective shield, similar to that being installed in South Korea and already installed in Israel. Technology exists which is currently able to shoot down 95% of all incoming missiles, but this will improve to take its reliability nearer 100%. We must aim to be able to destroy incoming missiles as near as possible to the launch site so any country thinking of launching them will know they are endangering their own people. We also want to invest in developing technology that can lock onto incoming missiles and redirect them into the sea.

Now nuclear weapons are in the hands of other states and there is a real risk they may proliferate further into non-state hands; the Mutually Assured Destruction idea doesn't work. We will still have much more focus on poverty alleviation and other life-giving projects for the common good than spending on weapons.

Assisting Poorer Countries

We believe in fair trade worldwide so that developing economies in the world can grow without competing with cheap subsidised products from elsewhere. This will need in some circumstances to be supplemented by Overseas Aid. Grinding poverty still holds 2.8 billion people around the world in its grip. For the Christian Peoples Alliance, poverty is not an accident. The CPA will therefore pursue policies including grant aid, loans and other forms of diplomacy and finance, so as to challenge the root causes of poverty, such as wars, generalised violence, persecution, human rights abuses, the arms trade, corrupt government, the crippling debt burden and unfair trade practices that distort the economies of poor countries.

Whilst maintaining our foreign aid budget at 0.7% of GDP we will refocus it on helping refugees and to ensure people don't become refugees. We will also ensure that the emphasis of our foreign aid is on development for the recipient's self-sufficiency, rather than rewarding inefficiency and corruption, or funding politically correct causes, by working in partnership with those organisations, charities and Governments that have shown themselves to be effective in utilising resources to achieve the maximum positive outcomes. The response to disasters such as that in the Philippines shows that the British people do care about those abroad that need help. We must be ready to extend a compassionate hand to anyone in our human family who needs it, wherever they are in the world.

Our Place in the World

We want a Britain that plays its full part in the world through the United Nations where we must maintain our permanent seat on the Security Council. We must be involved and give support to international peace agreements and international trade agreements. We must re-establish a close relationship with the Commonwealth and maintain the special relationship with the USA.

We will rebuild favourable trading relationships with any country in the world which wants to join with us in doing so to our mutual benefit provided they do not have an unacceptable human rights record. Prior to our membership of the EEC this was granted to Commonwealth countries and they will probably be the core of these new arrangements but not necessarily so. The reality is that before we joined the EEC, or the EU as it now is, we had a small trading surplus with the other EEC nations. After we joined that quickly became a large deficit. That means that our membership of the EU has been more beneficial to other

EU nations that it has been to the British. We want to be a country that plays its full part in the world and seeks trade agreements with the new economic powerhouses of China, Russia, India and Brazil as well as the emerging powerhouse of Africa. Trade with Europe may initially be diminished if we leave the EU but we will then be in a stronger position to increase our trade with the rest of the world, especially the Commonwealth. Over time there is no reason why we should not develop mutually beneficial trading relations with the EU as indeed Canada has done from far afield.

While persecution of Christians is being carried out so obviously and clearly by foreign Governments and non-Government bodies (including Boko Haram and Islamic State) we will give full support where we can to Christians and other faith groups who are being persecuted and offer them refuge wherever it is needed. We will seek international agreements to aid in their protection. All direct aid to Governments should be conditional on Christians and other faith groups not being persecuted. Thus, at present the UK Government is giving £441million in aid to Pakistan whilst, under law 295C of the Pakistan Penal Code, if anyone criticises the prophet Muhammad they have to be put to death (mandatory punishment). Thus Ms Asia Bibi was until recently on death row because she said, "Jesus Christ died for my sins, what has Muhammad ever done for you?" This cannot continue. Only on the release of Asia Bibi and with the repeal of this law can aid to Pakistan continue, and we would work with other governments and agencies to ensure freedom of religious expression and the human right to change one's religion here and throughout the world.

Israel

Israel is a small country in the heart of the Middle East surrounded by some very aggressive neighbours. Over the years these neighbours have three times tried to wipe it out in 1948, 1967 and 1973. There have been many attempts at peace most notably with Egypt and Jordan which have led to Israel returning land it had gained during wars in return for peace. It has also unilaterally withdrawn from the Gaza strip in an effort to make peace with the Palestinians. Despite all these efforts they have enemies committed to wiping them off the map.

*We assert the right of the nation of Israel to exist in peace, recognised by the PLA and Hamas.
*We assert the right of Palestinians, both Christian and Muslim, to live in peace
*We assert the duty of all people within Israel and without to engage in a democratic process to help bring peace in the region.

*We assert the duty of the international community to support Israel in promoting these rights and duties.

Greening the Economy and Transport

Although these are two separate matters they are closely interlinked, with our transport choices having a significant effect on the environment. Thus approximately 40,000 early deaths every year in the UK are currently attributable to nitrogen dioxide and particulates, primarily from diesel engines. However, in line with our principle of empowerment of local communities, transport strategies are primarily devolved to regional and local government.
At a national level the CPA would: -

*Institute a scrappage scheme for older diesel cars and vans.
*Encourage regional and local government to institute Ultra Low Emission Zones in city and town centres and in the vicinity of schools and hospitals as soon as possible and no later than 2020.
*Introduce the 'red, yellow, green' sticker system of car pollution identification and monitoring which has been shown to move motorists from high pollution cars (red stickers) to low pollution cars (green stickers).

*Consult on the introduction of car sharing lanes on busy motorways that may only be used by a car that has 3 or more occupants.

*Require all petrol stations to have an appropriate number of electric charging points.

*Encourage regional and local authorities to move to 100% electric taxis and private hire vehicles, with all new taxis, private hire vehicles to run on electric and new taxi and private hire licences to use electric vehicles.

*Encourage local transport authorities to move towards '100%' green buses by 2022.

*Invest in High Speed Rail to help revitalise the regions and eliminate internal air travel.

*Encourage regional and local authorities to physically separate cyclists and vehicles, have safer left-hand turns where appropriate and introduce traffic light priority for cyclists.

Greening the Economy

Whilst dealing with pollution by transport is a major part of greening the economy it is not all of it. Consequently, the CPA would also: -

*Consult on replacing subsidies so as to increase alternative electric production by solar, wind and tidal mechanisms at all levels (eg from solar panels on individual houses to large scheme tidal barrages).

*Consider funding research and development into better batteries and other electrical storage devices, again from house level to regional generators. This would be on the basis outlined at the end of the Brexit section of this Manifesto.

*Seek standardisation of recycling policies and materials across all local authorities.

*Impose a charge, similar to the 'carrier bag' charge on each item of non-recyclable packaging on any item sold. This will lead to manufacturers and consumers wanting fully recyclable packaging. The 'carrier bag' charge of 5p resulted in an initial drop of 85% from circa 7 billion in 12 months to 500 million in 6 months.

*Fund research into far greater use of recyclable materials e.g. utilising plastic in road construction

*Utilise our diplomatic and investment strategies to reduce deforestation and increase reforestation both abroad and at home.

*Review the UK's Climate Change Agreement and Climate Change Levy to ensure it is working effectively at reducing emissions whilst allowing energy intensive sectors of industry to work and compete effectively post-Brexit.

*Consult on the most cost-effective way of insulating all UK homes to cut down on heat loss and thus on energy bills.

*Keep to the Paris Agreement 2015 whilst working towards the first 5-year review in 2020, using our diplomatic, and foreign aid and investment strategies to that end.

*Operate a 'safety-first' or 'precautionary principle' to all pesticides and insecticides (including neo-nicotinoids) such that they may only be used once shown to be safe.
*Refuse licences for genetically modified foods.

Transport

With regard to air travel the CPA considers there has to be one large hub airport in the South of England. The CPA considers the ideal solution is to build a new hub airport in the Thames Estuary with 6 runways and linked to Crossrail and other rail networks. We totally accept that putting in sufficient transport links will take time. This will not be a fully operational 6 runway airport immediately. We will need to open one runway and then gradually put in the transport links until it is ready to be a full hub airport.

Sufficient initial work has already been done on design and costing by the Thames Estuary Research and Development Company. We will offer shares in the project and a bond to those who wish to lend money, as well as having a significant public share. This project will be integrated with the further regeneration of large parts of East London. When it is fully operational Heathrow will be scaled down or redeveloped for housing. The project is enormous but will also have vast rewards associated with it and make a plan that will maintain London as a primary international city for decades to come.

There are approximately 140,000 (2015) personal injury accidents a year, averaging just under 400 a day, with (an average) 69 serious injuries a day (2016) and 5 deaths a day (2016). Consequently, the CPA wants to take steps to improve road safety. We would immediately consult on a proposal that all vehicle drivers should be retested 5 years after first passing their test. Any driver shown to be unsafe will have to pay for a minimum of two additional driving lessons, a speed awareness course and a re-test following the lessons to have their full driving licence restored.

Any driver caught speeding or otherwise breaking the law and thereby have more than 9 points on their licence will have to pay for the lessons and course and re-test. Driving a half-ton of metal and glass on the roads, at speeds up to 30 mph or 70 mph is a privilege rather than a right and must be treated as such.

As with other road users (e.g. motorcyclists having helmets, car drivers & passengers wearing seatbelts) cyclists also have responsibility for their own wellbeing and the CPA will require: -

*Helmets of a suitable standard and luminosity to be worn.

*Clothing and backpacks to be worn of a suitable reflective luminosity for day and night (as appropriate).

*Lights, both front and rear, to be of an appropriate power and position so the cyclist will be seen, be able to be seen, but not 'blind' motorists.

In all cases we will consult on the actual standards to be adopted.

Reform the Banking System

Having debt based economic growth is bad for society. Debt is getting out of hand at all levels and measures must be taken to deal with it at all levels. See Appendix 2 for full statistics.

The Christian Peoples Alliance proposes to terminate the capacity of the banks to create money (known as 'fractional reserve banking'). All money loaned out must either come from repaid mortgages, savings or loans from the Bank of England.

We will consult on a limit on the amount of interest that can be charged on loans to, say, interest rates above 5% above the Bank of England Base Rate (currently 0.25%) or 10% whichever is the higher. This level to be subject to review. An institution that routinely charges the maximum level would be subject to scrutiny with the power of the

Regulatory Authorities to close it down. The aim of this is to tackle rogue lenders not good banks.

We will also: -

*Separate the banking roles between saving and lending and riskier investment banks.

*We will give the Bank of England the power to impose maximum multipliers for home mortgage loans and/or loan-to-value percentages. This will have the effect of dampening down (or increasing) house prices as is required by the economy and housing needs.

*We will consult on how the Bank of England can be made much more transparent in its dealings and how measures can be introduced to bring it under greater democratic control. One suggestion is a supervisory board independent of Government that has the power to see any Bank of England Documents and demand the reconsideration of a decision. The supervisory board would also have the power to interview Bank of England officials over any matter and veto appointments. The Supervisory Board could be called to account in the Administrative Court if it in turn overstepped its power. This accountability can and should be completely separate from the Government and at least some members should be elected. Others could be appointed by regulators.

The Treasury should launch its own cryptocurrency for use on line that is not tied to the Bank of England that can be a world currency leader. In years to come cryptocurrencies will become more and more important so we need to get in on the act now.

Immigration

It is essential we have a mature and balanced approach to this problem and avoid emotional rhetoric that can lead to racism and hatred of others. The Christian Democratic position is based on all of humanity being in God's Image (Imago Dei). This is not over-ridden by nationalism nor ethnicism which, themselves, lead to social discord. Consequently the CPA urges social peace within the global community and societal harmony within the UK.

The Christian Democratic position allows nationality change: indeed the UK has undergone many changes, such as Romanisation, Saxonisation and Normanisation. However, such changes must be by fair means not foul. Immigration must be fair.

Definitions

The term 'immigrant' defines someone who has permanently moved into a country, while migrant generally refers to someone who has entered an area (or country) from outside for a short term work or educational objective. There are numerous instances where official migrants remain without permission beyond their legal term and so become illegal immigrants. Whilst immigration has been of great benefit to our country, unrestricted immigration is unfair, both on existing citizens and those who seek to settle here by legitimate and legal means; and it's costs are considerable.

Consequently, the CPA immigration priorities are to provide a safe haven and to bring into the country those with the necessary skills who wish to live here. Once they have arrived CPA policy is that immigrants are to be treated as we treat our native born. That, however, is not, and should not, be, at the expense of the values, freedoms and culture of our society.

Statistical Reality

Population Density: England is the sixth most crowded country in the World. 1997-2010 showed a net immigration gain of about 2 million, with roughly 80% from non-EU countries, and figures project an extra net increase of 7 million by 2027, two-thirds of this by immigration. Approximately 45% of Londoners are now White British, down from 58% in 2001. Far right politics have been a reaction to fears of overcrowding and significant changes in the ethnic makeup of our population. The CPA takes both a realistic and grateful view of the natural and human resources that have come to the UK, and does not base citizenship rights on any racial grounds.

Refugees and Asylum Seekers

The Convention on Refugees 1951 (globalised by the 1967 Protocol) states that countries should offer first port of call shelter for those perceived to be fleeing from unjust persecution. If Port 1 is overloaded, subsequent ports should be open for fair distribution. The policies and actions of the UK Border Force must be audited for just ethical standards, including a proper up-to-date awareness of worldwide human rights issues, such as the way homosexuality or conversion to Christianity and other faiths can lead to serious persecution, including a death sentence, in many countries. We will give priority to those who have faced or may face persecution in such countries, consulting on those who have greatest need with preservation of life having the greatest priority.

Unaccompanied Children

We will also prioritise those unaccompanied children currently in France (especially the youngest and those who have family already residing in the UK) who are not receiving adequate shelter, protection or freedom from exploitation. We will consult on age appropriateness for those who should properly be considered 'children' for this policy.

In line with the Kindertransport principle (approx. 10,000 children) and treatment given by the UK to them we consider: -
*these children are vulnerable; and
*they are passing through a 'safe country'; and
*will, in due time, make a valuable and useful contribution to British society. So, having made their home here they should not be deported, once they have reached the age of eighteen, except in the case where the child has committed a serious crime.

The CPA will work with all appropriate statutory and voluntary agencies, including charities, to find appropriate adoptive and foster homes for those children. This programme will be 'until the crisis is over'.

Economic/Educational Immigrants

The UK needs guest workers due to declining and ageing populations. But it is unjust to take migrant professionals from developing countries to meet our own skills shortages, whether nurses, doctors or IT specialists. This long-term issue will be addressed by our policies to support marriage and family life to reverse the domestic de-population trend.

Until the declining birth rate is reversed, the CPA will use a UK version of the American Green Card system for determining who can come to work in Britain, based on the current 5 Tiers. The system is basically designed to assess how useful applicants are likely to be to the UK workforce, or how genuine their claim to student status is. Its Tier 3, designed to monitor low-skill short-term economic immigration, has never been used since the European Economic Area (EEA) visa-free door remains open to EU citizens. Until Brexit future EEA access should have a monitored condition which makes migrant workers and their sponsors responsible for housing and medical cover independent of the State. This will broaden accountability and encourage self-responsibility for those without current citizenship status, whilst reducing the burden on the taxpayer. After Brexit EEA access will be treated on the system as non-EEA access, as the CPA considers all humanity should be treated equally.

People Trafficking

The CPA would widely publicise an official mechanism to help immigrants enslaved (trafficked) without passport protection, and would, subject to the availability of funds, consider assisting those voluntary organisations who work in this field. Economic migrants can, by stolen passports, be enslaved, their wages stolen by traffickers, and also deprived of many of the protections relating to health, pay, housing, travel, and other welfare needs that many of us take for granted. They can end up homeless and completely disempowered.

Illegal Immigrants

There are an estimated 0.5 million illegal immigrants in the UK, mostly in London. The UK Border Agency is tasked with finding & deporting them: it is costly and time consuming. We should not be legitimising illegal immigration but ensuring that the system is fair for those who wish to live and work here legally, and for genuine asylum seekers.

We reject a one-off Qualified Amnesty. It may cause financial & social problems down the line. Crime should not pay. There inevitably has to be a time, however, when illegal immigrants have been here so long without committing any crime and without recourse to the State that they should be allowed to remain. We consider this point to be 10 years though there should be a further limit of 5 years for such people before State benefits can be claimed.

We will reward voluntary surrender by more sympathetic evaluation or free repatriation if required. This more sympathetic evaluation will be especially so where the person coming forward voluntarily has the support of a significant part of the local community relating to their positive commitment to society and thus for their continued residence in the UK. We will, however, punish concealment with tough penalties. Attrition through enforcement could make it harder to obtain benefits such as paid employment, medical care, and formal education, significantly reducing the size of the illegal population at reasonable cost by making re-immigration the best option. We will then pay for the air fares of those returning on the condition that it is understood they will never be allowed to visit the UK again unless the cost is refunded.

It is crucially important that the citizenship status of both parties to a marriage should be checked, and both parties fully warned about the possibility of illegal immigrants being denied a right to remain, before any wedding is conducted. Marriage should not be abused merely as a way of gaining citizenship status. However, there are valid marriages which are denied access to the UK by current rules, in particular 'the financial requirement'. This is currently £18,600 pa a year for a spouse with £3,800 for the first child and £2,400 for each subsequent child. Consequently, any British citizen who is on a low income or who has been working overseas for many years in an unpaid or low paid voluntary aid programme and has married overseas (whether with or without children) is unlikely to be able to return to the UK without leaving his wife and children behind. The CPA will consult on how this destructive policy on marriage may be rectified without allowing for the abuse of marriage for unlawful immigration.

We will greatly increase the efficiency and effectiveness in which our borders are managed. Outside of the EU this can be much more effective and fairer to all non-Britons wanting to come here.

Other Moral Issues

Whilst there is a moral element to all issues that are outlined in this manifesto there are some issues that are overwhelmingly of a moral nature. For the Christian Peoples Alliance, the issues below are absolutely central to what we stand for and the policies in this section are to promote family stability, respect for life and the effective use of resources to empower individuals and communities within a context of social justice.

The Importance of Marriage

Heterosexual marriage remains the fundamental building block for a healthy society, and the safest environment for the bringing of children into the world. Statistically, very few horror stories of child abuse come from married households (Robert Whelan's Broken Homes & Battered Children, 1994, Family Education Trust). The Christian Peoples Alliance has detailed proposals to strengthen marriage and encourage its stability. Failure to do so cheapens lives, removes the sacred. Even financially, defending marriage makes sense, as Government figures show that marriage breakdowns cost the country almost £50 billion each year. What seems lacking is the political will to call marriage right, and interpersonal sex outside marriage as wrong in itself, and damaging.

Research shows that many couples are unprepared for marriage and parenting. We therefore have detailed proposals to strengthen marriage and encourage its stability and improve parenting.

First, we would give a grant (initially set at £12,000 per couple) to be made available to all couples on the occasion of their first marriage provided that they go for at least 5 sessions of marital awareness training.

Second, we would give a grant (initially set at £6,000) to be made available to all before or just after the birth or adoption of their first child provided they go for at least 5 sessions of training in child raising as the child is the priority.

Third, we want the tax threshold to be fully transferable from husband to wife if there is a child under 5 in the family so that there is a tax benefit for one parent to stay at home with young children. Equally there will be an incentive for the other parent to look for work when the youngest child reaches age 5. As resources make it possible, we will extend this age limit preferably right up to age 12.

Fourth, we will allow married couples to name 2 properties as their main home, one each, to end the Capital Gains tax anomaly where unmarried couples are better off.

The reason for these measures is that research has shown that too many couples are sliding into marriage without properly thinking about what they are doing. Equally many parents receive little or no training and so do not cater for the needs of their children as they should. The whole of society will benefit from a change of culture which these measures will bring about.

One Christian leader stated regarding marriage, "at stake is the identity and survival of the family: father, mother and children. At stake are the lives of many children who will be discriminated against in advance and deprived of their human development given by a father and a mother and willed by God. At stake is the total rejection of God's law engraved in our hearts." (Pope Francis) Another said "Marriage is like a structural wall in a building. If we destroy marriage the whole of society can come crashing down." (Jonathan Olyede of the Global Day of Prayer)
Whilst looking to strengthen marriage we will not remove the legal concept of 'civil partnership' although we will consult on finding a better name for this form of committed relationship.

Adoptive families

The CPA believes adoptive parents make a highly significant contribution to the lives of the children they adopt and to the community as a whole. They provide a home for a child (or children) in need and may end a cycle of abuse and/or neglect within families. Potentially they save a lot of social work costs and so they need and deserve support from government at all levels.

The CPA believes every effort should be made to ensure that once a child is placed with adoptive parents the placement succeeds. The cost of an adoption placement breakdown both in terms of emotional damage to the child and to the wider community should be avoided if at all possible.

Therefore, we propose

1.   When advertising for new adoptive parents it should be recognised by government at all levels that a child's problems (such as learning difficulties, Attachment Disorder, ADHD, autism spectrum disorders, foetal alcohol syndrome or the effects of physical or sexual abuse) do not disappear because the child is moved into an adoptive family.

2.   Post-adoption support staff should be actively encouraged to assist adoptive parents in matters such as school placements, even when this requires them to openly disagree with their employers.

3.	Every school should be encouraged to have a specific policy with regard to 'looked after' and adopted children that recognises the unique needs of this group and sets out how these will be addressed in the school situation. (The views of agencies such as Adoption UK and similar groups may be considered when policies are made.) Reports by Ofsted on schools and other institutions should include an assessment of how well the body concerned meets the needs of 'looked after' and adopted children.

4.	Civil servants who have contact with adoptive parents should recognise the contribution the parents have made not just to their children but to the community as a whole. This contribution is often made at a very real cost to the parents concerned. The notion of 'win/win' whereby the community is seen as benefiting from the child being moved out of 'care' and the adoptive parents as benefiting by getting the child they want should be actively challenged and dismissed.

5.	Courses in colleges and Universities for the training of teachers, health professionals, social workers and others from the caring professionals should cover how to meet the unique needs of adopted children and their families. Wherever possible relevant agencies such as Adoption UK and similar should be included in the development of policies and training programmes.

6.   Churches and other community groups should be encouraged to support adoptive families wherever possible.

7.   Local authorities and other adoption agencies should be required to maintain a record of how many of the children they place with adoptive parents remain with those parents and how many are returned to 'care'.

When an adoption placement fails there should be a full investigation by the local authority. This investigation should lead to a report giving reasons for the placement failure and recommendations for future practice. It should be submitted to the department of the relevant minister of state.   A summary of these reports should be presented annually to Parliament along with recommendations for any legislative or other changes that may be considered necessary. If the adoptive parents are not satisfied with the investigation, then they should have the right to appeal to an independent inspector appointed by central government giving their reasons.

We would provide more respite centres for families experiencing breakdown and easy access to counselling and training in child rearing free of charge to anyone who wants to commit to participating in it.

Our concern is focussed on the needs of children and we should be doing all we can to rebuild a society where children live with their natural parents and, where that fails, in a safe, secure and welcoming adoptive family. Of course, full help and support must and will be given to lone parents but not at the expense of seeking to solve the reason why families are breaking down in the first place.

There can and should be state recognition for other mutually supportive relationships where two people have lived together for a long time, including siblings, so that inheritance can be passed between them and they can be named "next of kin". We have opposed all attempts to redefine the meaning of marriage and will repeal those laws which have already attempted to do this. We will not, however, take away the legal rights of same sex couples other than the right to call their relationship "marriage" and their right to adopt children as we believe children are always better off with a father and a mother and the interests of children should come first.

Schools should not be used as an apparatus for social engineering and promoting the secular liberal agenda. They should respect the views of parents and the cultural background of pupils. Schools must not be able to take action against teachers who support real marriage, and neither should any employer, government or otherwise be able to take action on this basis.

Further Family Support

In order to give additional support to the family we will: -

*Restore Sunday as a day of rest and family time. We will make it obligatory to close most retail outlets by limiting the numbers that can be employed on any premises to 5 people on a Sunday, at Easter and at Christmas. We will also make it obligatory for government and local authority workers to be given the day off on Sunday if they want it and we will normally make it illegal to include compulsory Sunday working in any contract of employment.

*Make available free of charge counselling for drug addiction and alcohol addiction, treating the addict as a patient rather than a criminal, and ensuring a 24-hour emergency service is provided for urgent methadone or similar prescription to help individuals and families cope with the terrible pressures that come through drug misuse.

*Tackle child poverty by introducing new child tax allowances of £2,373 per child to all parents up to 5 per family. The cost of this has been estimated at £4 billion.

*Allow parents who stay at home to receive enhanced child benefit in the early years to encourage parents to spend more time with very young children.

Youth Policy

Britain's youth unemployment was around 13% at the end of last year. Changes to the welfare state for unemployed under 25's is creating a sense of hopelessness among some who have nowhere to turn from age 18 to 25.

At the same time the cost of living has increased albeit at a slower rate, but it is still rising while a lack of discipline in society has led young people to resort to loan sharks as a first option to manage bills. So also when the far right blames all society's problems on immigration it encourages racism and a class hatred among the youth and even a gang psychology.

There are alarming reports of children engaging in emotional and physical abuse towards their parents and society so that it seems the breakdown of moral signposts from a very young age has become a norm. It is known this is part of the liberal agenda described in chapter 2.

The CPA proposes: -

*To reinforce and strengthen programmes to ensure unemployment is not an option for any young person. We want to see more resources allocated to encourage apprentice schemes and voluntary placements which can lead to full time employment after a period. These placements must not be motivated by greed for 'financial sweeteners' nor cheap labour but the desire to give a young person a chance. Rogue employers will be weeded out.

*We want young people to have community mentors who can help them make the right decisions. The ethos of loving our neighbour has almost become outdated whereby we may not even know who are living on our streets. If young people are engaged with their community then it encourages safer neighbourhoods and involvement with the elderly so they feel supported. We need more community spirit and less division. We want these community schemes to operate outside the police or social services.

These policies are also designed to empower the young within the context of increasing the quality of social justice within our society.

The sanctity of life from conception to natural death

No life is unimportant or not worth living. The abortion statistics in the UK are a national tragedy. Around 9 million unborn children have lost their lives to abortion since the passing of the 1967 Abortion Act. In 2017 alone, for women resident in England and Wales, the total number of abortions was 194,668.

The Christian Peoples Alliance is unashamed to declare its commitment to the principle of respect for life. God values everyone equally and so every citizen from conception (fertilisation) to natural death deserves the protection of the law. The language of human rights is often heard in both our national and the European Parliament, but rarely that of the most basic human need – to be born, nurtured and protected without fear of death in utero. Abortion leads to increased exploitation of women, not their 'liberation'. Abortion violates the dignity and integrity of women. It leaves a trail of anger, guilt, resentment, depression and loss of self-respect. Whenever we act or speak, we pledge to do so, however, without judging or condemning any individual, especially any woman who has been involved in abortion. The Biblical basis for opposing abortion was discussed in chapter 2.

This compassionate Christian approach also requires that we speak up for those who, because of age or infirmity, are perceived in many European states to be a burden on others and will strongly oppose the growing euthanasia culture. EU member states which proclaim their commitment to equal opportunities for disabled adults often ignore their duty to afford equal protection to disabled pre-born human beings. They have adopted a double standard. We will use our voice in Parliament to challenge these primitive prejudices and fears concerning disability. Negative and defeatist, deeply insulting to the born disabled, eugenic abortion also causes severe trauma to the mother.

There are already demographic consequences of an anti-life culture. With birth-rates falling dangerously below replacement levels, we now face major economic and social problems associated with an ageing population. The issue of live birth-rate in turn has implications for the question of migration. States which kill their unborn and do not support marriage and family life, are having to replace this missing workforce through liberalising the numbers of people they admit, with inevitable issues relating to integration.

Much western aid to developing countries is ruthlessly anti-life, with tens of millions of taxpayers' money being spent on promoting abortion and sterilisation in China, Bangladesh and elsewhere. The CPA deplores such 'aid' programmes: they do not provide solutions to poverty but merely export our 'culture of death' to countries struggling to develop their economies.

In Parliament, we pledge ourselves to a nation in which all citizens enjoy equal status, in which the extended family is reinforced as the bedrock of social structure, where motherhood is once again respected, and where we use with wisdom the fruits of new scientific discoveries.

MPs for the CPA therefore pledge to:

*Allow those who have philosophical or moral objections to abortion to be able to conscientiously object into the processes leading to abortion.
*Step by step repeal the 1967 Abortion Act.
*Challenge the culture of death by seeking legislation which confers the full protection of the law on all human life from conception until natural death.
*Ensure recognition for the millions of women who have had abortions. Post-abortion trauma affecting many women must now be recognised and non-judgemental post-abortion

counselling will be made available for any woman who wants it, no matter how long ago the abortion took place.

*End the practises of cloning, embryo experimentation and all reproductive technologies which lead to the intentional destruction of human life.

*Support legislation to prevent the patenting of natural genetic material, modifications to the human germline and the trade in sperm, ova and human beings at the embryonic stage of development.

*Outlaw voluntary, non-voluntary and involuntary euthanasia by omission or by direct act, including neonatal euthanasia and euthanasia of patients in a 'persistent vegetative state'.

*Seek the nationwide provision of pro-life pregnancy care services, including provision of accommodation for women made homeless by pregnancy, pregnant women with special needs and one-parent families.

*International aid will be ended to any agency or government which promotes abortion, euthanasia or forced sterilisation programmes, coercive contraception or other violations of human rights (e.g. arbitrary imprisonment or deportation, slavery, or sale of women or children).

*Enable additional work to take place between the NHS and the voluntary sector to increase the provision of good quality terminal and palliative and respite care for infants, children and adults, whether in their own homes or in hospices. This care will be benchmarked against the world's best examples of each.

Care for the less able

It is obviously desirable to get people off benefit into work if at all possible. However, we will exempt from this drive:-

*Anyone who is physically disabled to the extent that they need assistance to move around.

* Anyone who is registered mentally disabled and has not been completely discharged.

* We will remove the test of being "able to do any work" and replace it with the test "able to work in an occupation which the applicant is suited to perform." If it is deemed by a doctor that an applicant previously able to receive benefits is now "able to work in an occupation which the applicant is suited to perform" then we will not cease benefits until a job offer is actually made or until the applicant misses 3 interviews for jobs or at a job centre without reasonable cause. We will end the injustices portrayed in the recent film "I, Daniel Blake".

* If an appeal is made against a decision to remove benefits those benefits will be kept in place until the appeal is heard. (These benefits include the current provision of a motability car).

In addition, we will introduce a new rule that anyone who applies for benefits is given immediate help if there is a reasonable prospect that their application will be successful. This help will only be required to be paid back if it is shown that there has been serious dishonesty in the application and the authorities were misled. This should mean that the days when job centres are sending applicants to food banks are over.

Issues relating to those on Low Incomes, including the Elderly

It is easy to assume that things cannot change for the British workforce. But it is possible, relatively quickly, to change the work patterns of substantial numbers of people for the better. Working with business organisations, unions and employers' forums, the Christian Peoples Alliance will seek to increase the income those in the poorest sectors of society get. It will also identify ways of overcoming problems related to over-work, so that time is released for people to spend in rest and recreation and in developing relationships, especially with older relatives and with children.

We will review the minimum wage set at £7.50 per hour from April 2017 for adults over 25. The CPA aims to increase this to the current Real Living Wage of £8.45 per hour outside London and £9.75 per hr in London for all aged 18 and over as soon as practically possible following consultation. We believe this is a key factor in our drive to care for the poor and reduce poverty.

We will make Zero Hours contracts illegal except for employees under 21 or over 65. These distort the workforce by tying someone to a job from which they may be receiving no income at all and makes it very hard for them to find other work. Agencies are available for employers to get workers at short notice. The only reason for zero hours contracts is to have a reserve of cheap labour. It must stop. Where Zero Hrs contracts do continue for the under 21s or over 65s anyone called in must be paid for at least 2 hours work.

Where benefits are used to avoid taking responsibility and finding work then they can be counter productive to the community, but we will always make sure that the poorest are cared for.

Christians have long been involved in many initiatives 'on the ground' in their communities, including foodbanks, debt counselling, and practical care for people on the streets. Low wages are not the only cause of poverty and we will always look for ways to help people who need help for whatever reason. We don't just talk good policies we act them out whether or not we are elected to public office. In everything we do we will seek to support all initiatives from the voluntary sector, including those from charities that help the poorest in our society.

For the elderly and severely disabled we will make it mandatory for Local Authorities to keep a full record of elderly and disabled citizens in their borough and to make an assessment of their risk to floods, snow, extreme weather or to natural disasters. Support must be put in place to ensure that those least able to care for themselves are looked after in the community and that full support is given to carers, especially those who are close relatives and tend to be forgotten.

The full new State Pension is currently £159.55. As finances allow the CPA will increase this to £200 per week at current prices but there after the CPA would keep a double lock – the higher of increase in inflation or average earnings but would remove the minimum increase of 2.5% a year. For once the pensioned have a reasonable figure on which to live it is not right that there is a transfer of resources (in real terms) from the young to the old that is greater than either average earnings or the rate of inflation.

The National Insurance record is used to calculate the new State Pension. 10 qualifying years are usually needed to get any new State Pension. The amount paid can be higher or lower depending on National Insurance records. It will only be higher if you have over a certain amount of Additional State Pension. We welcome these changes which finally put to bed all the argument over SERPS.

In general, we consider the idea to allow people to cash in previously purchased annuities to be an ill thought out gimmick and do not support it. However there should be an exception for those who have annuities paying out small amounts, say less than £100 per month. Such amounts should not be offset against benefits.

Morally Framed Education

A child's education is the prime responsibility of its parents which it is the duty of Government not to undermine. As Christian Democrats we oppose encroaching interference by the State in the content of the curriculum often in a very liberal and immoral way. As a result, the content of the National Curriculum has become a key battle ground and it is set to become even more of a battle ground in the future.

The Christian Peoples Alliance says: -
There should be no change in the current school structure with a mixture of private, state and voluntary schools. The issue is about increasing the quality of educational outcome, not the means by which that is delivered. To this end money must be spread equally across all schools, not favouring any one type of school. Where there is an imbalance in funding that must be addressed by increasing resources to those who lack but without taking away from existing providers.

Education means teaching all points of view, otherwise it becomes indoctrination, not education. Sadly today too much of our education is beginning to fall into the indoctrination category. It is not the aim of CPA to indoctrinate something different but to educate properly.

Most notably: -

*Religious Education must explain what both the adherents of the religion believe in a clear way and it is good practice for adherents of a religion to be invited into a school to explain their views. At the same time children should also be taught what critics of a religion teach and this must apply to all religions, Christian, Muslim, Hindu, Buddhist etc.

*Sex education should teach both Christian values of marriage between a man and a woman for life and the need to preserve one's sexual organs for marriage and also the secularist view of having sex when you want it but using condoms to prevent disease.   All children approaching puberty should know about sexually transmitted diseases and how and when they can be caught. What other religions teach about marriage should also be explained.

*As well as the more secularist concept of 'human rights', children will be taught the concepts of good and evil, right and wrong, morality and immorality enabling them to choose by which moral code they wish to live.

*When teaching history great care should be taken to express history from different perspectives and also to teach history which is relevant to the child. For instance, it is important that children learn about recent wars as well as British history from 1066. When talking about history children need to know the good and the bad and understand how the people at the time on different sides were feeling and what motivated them, not just the facts and the outcome.

*The idea of macroevolution should be taught as the majority position of the scientific community. However, the strength of Intelligent Design, which caused the long-term leading atheist Antony Flew to side with Einstein and Aristotle in acknowledging God as universal creator, should be outlined. Flew's book, "There Is A God", should be strongly recommended to all entrusted to teach science.

Parents should always have the right to know the details of the curriculum in their children's school and to withdraw their children from certain classes if they wish. Teachers should be encouraged to teach from different perspectives not just their own, but they should have the right to express their views as well as teaching the views of others. The idea that a Christian teacher cannot say that they are a Christian and why they are a Christian is wrong, but they have to understand and also teach the secular viewpoint. Equally a secularist or homosexual teacher should be able to say they are secular or homosexual but understand and teach the Christian point of view

Christian worship in all schools was part of the 1944 Education Act. Today the CPA believes that all children should know what Christian worship is and the role it plays in our society. To get a full understanding they must participate in it and be encouraged to engage themselves if they wish to. However, parents should equally always have the right to say they do not want their children to participate in Christian or other worship or any other religious activity.

Christian schools should be encouraged and if appropriate state funded but every effort should be made to ensure a broad curriculum in these schools and that other points of view are taught. If this is not the case, then state funding should be withdrawn. Schools set up with a clear religious ethos should have the right to set their own admission policies. However, if admission policies are set too narrowly then State funding may not be appropriate. These schools need to be the subject of a review, taking into account such matters as support for violence, attitudes towards women and towards those of other faiths if their people wish to convert. Whilst schools with either a secularist or a religious ethos have a right to exist, indoctrination should never be allowed to operate in British schools.

As far as school structures are concerned, we will do all we can to provide a stable educational environment for children and where possible reduce class sizes. Stability is vital in education and constant changes leave children feeling insecure. Too many structural changes have been taking place over the past 20 or so years. At the same time the more individual attention children get, especially those with special needs, the better.

For Universities the CPA wants open debate on all issues and to encourage close relationships between Universities and the world of work. Our universities should increasingly become national debating centres and State funding should be given to encourage this process with certain debates and lectures being open to people from outside the University to come and participate. The CPA wants an open and free society where ideas can be expressed, and no-one lives in fear of expressing them.

The CPA is in principle opposed to tuition fees which are saddling young people with debt from an early age. We will immediately consult on how we can increase funding for Universities and maintain and increase student numbers without tuition fees so long as access to Universities by the poorest in society is not thereby reduced.

Integration Agenda

The CPA believes totally in the freedom of religion. We will address all issues relating to other religions by encouraging and sponsoring national debate on the rights and wrongs of different religions. We will encourage the best minds in the world to come and take part in televised debates and encourage those debates to continue in our schools and Universities. Under the Christian Peoples Alliance there will be freedom to change religion for anyone at any time and freedom for anyone to express their views in a rational non-violent way. We believe this is the process that will undermine and destroy Islamic radicalism more than any other. We will, however, at the same time keep a very careful eye on any one individual or organisation that supports hatred and violence and if necessary, proscribe the organisation as illegal in the UK.

We would stop all state support for any organisations in the UK for which opposition to Christianity is part of their creed. We will give full support where we can to Christians and other faith groups who are being persecuted and offer them refuge wherever it is needed. We will seek international agreements to aid in their protection.

The CPA does not believe in state control of what people wear so we would not ban the burqa. There is widespread concern about the operation of religious courts in the UK. The CPA believes their operation should be reviewed and, if need be, regulated–to ensure they operate in accordance within the basic concepts of British jurisprudence. A parallel legal system can be very dangerous and should only exist if the judgements made are reasonable, a necessary part of the religion and within the basic concepts of British jurisprudence.

We believe these policies are in accord with the principle of social justice.

Crime, Punishment and Restorative Justice

For a real and lasting reduction in crime we need to tackle its' root causes. If Christian values of loving neighbours, loving enemies and forming lasting stable relationships are followed perfectly then real crime will cease. However simply by promoting those values crime will reduce. The by-product of this will be safer streets, better parenting and a happier society. Our aim is to eliminate the yob culture and the "me first" society.

Relationships are absolutely key when we are talking about crime. Stable relationships of love and caring are needed in every society and are the fundamental basis of a Christian community. Of course, everyone at some time in their life will make mistakes. When this happens as a society we should look first at restoration and only second at punishment. At the moment too easily, we arrest people and bang them up in a police cell or jail without making any attempt to understand why the so called crime has been committed or what is happening. This frequently causes resentment and anger and needs to change to a process of ask questions first and seek to resolve a problem and arrest only as a last resort.

Where the criminal justice system has to be involved the central goal of the Christian Peoples Alliance is to repair the relationship between the offender and victim. This process ensures that victims can tell offenders the real impact of their crime and hopefully receive an apology. Offenders have a chance to understand the real impact of what they've done and do something to repair the harm. They will also have a chance to explain their motive to the victim and explain why they did what they did while at the same time they are held to account. Notwithstanding this helping the victim is central to the process. There is research which shows that this is the best way to reduce crime and anti-social behaviour, reduce re-offending rates and has the by-product of cost savings and less fear of crime. This is not done in isolation and is not a soft option, people can still be sent to jail, but we would make it a vital part of the criminal justice system.

We are very keen to re-invigorate Neighbourhood Watch Schemes and these will be properly funded. At the same time support for Street pastors and special constables will support the community approach. CPA policies are to invest in social institutions which encourage a law-abiding lifestyle and especially to support the family.

At the moment half of all offenders go on to recommit crime so at the moment the prison system on its own simply isn't working. New initiatives are desperately needed. In addition to the restorative Justice system outlined above we will also: -

*Launch a "pathway out of the life of crime" initiative to help parents whose children have been lured into crime. This will be linked in with our overall policy to support marriage and the family outlined above.
*We will take a stricter approach to drug use because of the clear link between drug use and crime.

*We will restore local authority licensing of the sale of alcohol and repeal the 24-hour licensing legislation to seek to reduce the number of alcohol related offences and the number of people who become alcoholics.

*We will increase the resources being spent on vocational courses in prisons to give prisoners the best possible chance of working when they are released. Studies in America have shown that those who acquire vocational qualifications in prison are 33% less likely to offend.

*The Gambling Act 2005 will be repealed, and new controls put on Casinos with mandatory warnings having to be placed in all betting shops that gambling can cause serious poverty. We will ban the advertising of all gambling just as the advertising of smoking has been prohibited.

*We will oppose any attempts to relax moral laws such as legalising brothels or legalising prostitution. This undermines the welfare of society as a whole by treating women as sexual playthings rather than objects of real love and affection which they are meant to be.

*We want the recommendations of Ian Acheson on radicalisation in prisons implemented in full. This is a very serious problem which needs constant monitoring. The CPA will ensure that all prison officers get appropriate training to spot radicalisation. We will also train them in countering it through effective debate.
*We will consult on the introduction of mobile telephone and drone frequency blocking technology, preventing these in use in, or close by, prisons.

Under the CPA there will be freedom to leave or change religion for anyone at any time, and freedom for anyone to express their views in a non-violent way. Interference with those freedoms will be treated as 'hate-crime'. There will, however, be no tolerance or acceptance of any individual or organisation that supports hatred and violence and we will if necessary, proscribe any such organisation as illegal in the UK.

Social Media providers will be treated as 'publishers' not 'platforms' of any pornographic or violent material, or material promoting violent or otherwise illegal activity, such that they will become criminally liable for publishing it.

Human trafficking is an issue that has arisen in recent years and the authorities have been very slow to get to grips with it. Also called "modern slavery" the CPA will increase resources to see it stamped out for good.

The three-year limit on any civil claim for damages, whether financial, physical or psychological due to criminal activity would be lifted. There is no reason why, because a criminal wins the lottery or receives an inheritance or similar more than 3 years after committing the crime that they should still be free of any obligation to recompense their victim (for the injury or damage caused, no matter how long before).

A recognition that, when a life is taken, whether accidentally or on purpose, that something significant has happened. We propose a payment of minimum £100,000, depending on the circumstances payable by the person or organisation causing the death as a 'life compensation'. That is not to say this is the value of a life but that with their death something significant has taken place and that must be recognised by all concerned. It may be paid by the individual, their family, employee or insured against (public liability). It will rest against the person causing death and against their estate (but no further) and survives bankruptcy.

We will consider the results of any consultation on the Money Laundering Regulations so as to ensure that these are truly effective in dealing with crime and money laundering whilst not imposing unnecessary regulatory burdens on small businesses. At present they do not seem to be effective whilst causing undue time and cost on the businesses that have to implement them.

We make 3 further proposals relating to Extra Territorial Sovereignty: -

*Anyone who harms a British Citizen abroad may be brought back to the UK for trial.

*Any British Citizen who acts illegally abroad can be tried in the UK (including consideration by the Attorney General and referral to the Court of Appeal if sentence abroad was too light).

*We would make sure all sex offenders convicted abroad are made to sign the Sex Offenders Register on return.

Housing and Development

The breakdown of families and marriage coupled with increased immigration has together put the need for housing in our society under increased strain.

The first resort is not just to build more houses but to address some of the underlying causes of the increased need. This we have done elsewhere in this manifesto. Coupled with this where wealth has increased there is also an increased likelihood that some people will own both a working home in a city and a rest home of some sort away from a city.

Despite this even while the underlying causes are being addressed there will still be a need for more houses to be built. The CPA proposes: -

The process of encouraging more new housing to be built in city centres will be increased. As shopping habits are changing and more people are either buying on line or going to out of town shopping centres, old city centres can be re-invigorated by building as much housing as possible in city centres which will include new shops with flats above them. This housing is useful for anyone who does not want a garden, particularly young people, and in many cases reduces travel requirements so easing congestion on road and rail. It also helps the shopping centres themselves by increasing the number of people who live nearby and does away with places that are dead at night.

We would reform the Section 106 procedure to ensure that all new private housing schemes, where required would have an element, or payment towards, new affordable or socially rented housing provision.
Unused development areas will be identified, and significant new sites will be made available for housing.

In an area where there are a significant number of empty houses if these cannot be brought back into use we will look at redevelopment to improve and invigorate an area. This will sometimes be painful in the short term but will always have long term benefits.

We will ensure that 90% of housing is CO_2 neutral by 2050 through housing developments that are carbon neutral and by taking further measures to encourage the insulation of existing houses.
We will do our level best to avoid turning green sites into housing estates. This should only happen as an exception.

Second Homes to be a different use class in planning to main residence (to protect rural communities) with automatic planning permission for reversion from Second Home status to Main Residence status, but not the other way round. This will lead to an increase in current Second Home values rising faster than Main Residence values in the same area (as the supply of Second Homes is restricted), but that can be addressed, if need be, through Capital Gains Tax.

There is an urgent need for good quality and affordable move-on accommodation (for those coming out of homelessness) to be provided using a mixture of voluntary, private and state sponsored provision. As with other matters in this Manifesto it is about the quality of the provision, rather than who is the provider

There is also an urgent need to reform the Leasehold Reform legislation by which people may purchase the freeholds or extend their leases on their homes. This now dates back up to 50 years and is no longer fit for purpose.

The CPA would: -

*Remove the concept of 'marriage value' from all lease extensions and freehold purchases. In relatively simple cases, of leases of less than 50 years outside of Prime Central London this will reduce the cost to leaseholders by up to £100,000.

*Reduce the complexity of the timetabling of all claims and remove all the 'traps' in the legislation (to prevent the 'game-playing' of solicitors) resulting in a far simpler process, reduced costs and fewer professional indemnity claims.

*Reform the 'commercial' system so it is workable and require all new blocks of flats and blocks where the leaseholders purchase the freehold to be on the new revised commercial basis.

*Consult on bringing all leases of residential property under consumer legislation rather than just land law legislation, such that unfair terms in the lease can be voided by the courts. In particular, the CPA would introduce legislation such that all leases where ground rents increase by more than double every 25 years become a fixed ground rent for the remaining length of the lease.

The Political Process

The CPA considers that the following reforms to our political process are currently needed: -

*All voters should provide proof of identity when voting to avoid impersonation.

*We support the right of recall by the electorate of any sitting MP as it now operates.

*We would consult on the introduction of proportional representation for all local elections.

*We would reform the House of Lords, with all members of the Second Chamber being elected by Proportional Representation with no lower threshold. This would mean that a party gaining just 1% of the vote would probably get 3 seats if there are 300 members and ensure a wide range of views are represented with it being very unlikely one party would control the chamber.

Developing a Christian Manifesto

CHAPTER 7
Where do we go from here?

"If you can dream - and not make dreams your master;
If you can think - and not make thoughts your aim;
If you can meet with Triumph and Disaster
And treat those two impostors just the same..."

Rudyard Kipling

Where do we go from here?

We believe God's plan is that this manifesto forms the policy of the Government of the United Kingdom. So how will it work?

We are determined to lay a foundation that cannot be shaken, the foundation of the apostles and prophets hearing the word of the Lord and acting out the strategies He gives. The foundation is already laid. God is bringing the people in. In 2015 we had 17 candidates. In 2017 we had 31 candidates. We are getting more and more lined up, but we need 500 to be an option for Government. That is where you come in.

We need candidates to stand in the next General Election in your town or city. We're not content to stand again covering just 5% of all constituencies. We have the manifesto. Now we need the people to stand with us. Then we need agents to stand alongside the candidates and offer their support. Jesus never sent people out in ones. He sent them out two by two. Some are meant to speak, they are the candidates. Others are meant to be there in support. They are the agents who manage the campaign for the candidates.

If you are called to play either role get in touch via e mail sidcordle@yahoo.co.uk. Then we need prayer warriors to stand alongside the candidates and agents. This is a battle for God against the strategy of Satan. Satan will resist us with all his might, but God is stronger. However, we need all the spiritual forces at our disposal. We can only win this battle equipped with the whole armour of God and then performing the task God gives us to perform. "And pray in the Spirit on all occasions with all kinds of prayers and requests. With this in mind, be alert and always keep on praying for all the Lord's people. Pray also for me, that whenever I speak, words may be given me so that I will fearlessly make known the mystery of the gospel, for which I am an ambassador in chains. Pray that I may declare it fearlessly, as I should." (Eph 6:18-20). You pray and seek God. So in every constituency we will have a candidate, an agent and a prayer warrior and then we will be ready for the battle.

How long will it take? I have said on many occasions. It's fine for me if I lay the foundation and others come after me who will build on that foundation and take the CPA to Government. It doesn't matter to me how long it takes. What matters is we get there, and we move forward at the speed God calls us to move with our eyes fixed on the calling.

Please don't think someone else will do this. You are called to play one of these 3 roles. If you work for the Government, you can only be a prayer warrior. If you work for yourself or in private industry you can be a candidate or an agent. Please put this book down and pray now. A very powerful passage in the Bible is Ezek 22v29,30, "The people of the land practice extortion and commit robbery; they oppress the poor and needy and mistreat the foreigner, denying them justice. I looked for someone among them who would build up the wall and stand before me in the gap on behalf of the land..." God is looking for someone who will stand in the gap on behalf of the UK to claim authority in this nation. God doesn't need thousands of people. Just 300 stood with Gideon and that was enough, but God is looking for people who are totally committed. Please pray now what your role should be. It is not by accident you have read this book.

ABOUT THE AUTHOR

Sid Cordle is leader of the Christian Peoples Alliance and is a sought-after conference speaker. He first stood for Parliament in 1983 as a Conservative Candidate and has stood many more times since. He spent six years as a Conservative Councillor in Sheffield before leaving the party in 2004. For ten years from 2005 he went down regularly to Speakers Corner in London where he engaged in polemics and apologetics often speaking alongside Jay Smith. As a keen runner he excelled for his club and in the Great North Run and London marathon. He is married to Bukky. They are jointly blessed with 7 children from previous marriages and he now also has 3 grandchildren. They are both active in Christian ministry in various leadership roles.

Contact: sidcordle@gmail.com telephone +(44)020 8855 8027

Where do we go from here?

Printed in Great Britain
by Amazon